The Longing For Belonging

Giving Up Ashes To Find Beauty

BRIDGET ANDERSON

Beauty for Ashes Publishing

Copyright © 2021 by Bridget Anderson

All rights reserved. This book or any portion thereof may not be reproduced or used in any manner whatsoever without the express written permission of the publisher except for the use of brief quotations in a book review.

Printed in the United States of America

ISBN: 978-0-578-88881-1

Acknowledgements

To God my Father, I thank You for giving me my story, where You knew I would find You.

To my precious family, my husband Wayne and my daughters Lainey and Emmy, I thank you for putting up with chicken nugget dinners, a not-so-clean house, and for not minding all the time I spent tucked away at Panera and in the basement writing this book. Thank you for your endless encouragement and for the honest and tough editing from Emmy. Your help was invaluable! You three are the best of my life!

To my parents Bart and Francie Murphy, I thank you for all you gave to your family.

To my sisters, Marie and Kellie, I thank you for being my steadfast companions, for sharing an unusual sense of humor with me, and with whom I have an unbreakable bond.

To AMTC I thank you for revealing to me how big our God is and inspiring me to dream big.

And to all the friends who have become my family, especially Ruthie, Crystal, Joanie, Melissa M., Mary, Lorrie, Kathy, Renee, and Angela. I thank you for being part of my life and for all that you bring to it.

"... He will give a crown of beauty for ashes, a joyous blessing instead of mourning, festive praise instead of despair ..."

Isaiah 61:3

And So It Began...

Bamboozled. Hoodwinked. Swindled.

Call it what you will, but I see clearly now that I had believed an outrageous lie and all that went along with it!

I believed I was not loved by God. Some people were, yes, but I was not. And I believed all the lies that fell from this main one. I had been left on my own. God was angry and tired of waiting on me to measure up to His standards. Instead of waiting to bless me, I knew a "Father" who was biding His time, until it was time for Him to quietly contort my life again with the next round of punishment. ba

I had a hole in my heart and a fiery ball in my throat that couldn't be extinguished. These manifestations of anxiety stemmed from the inconceivable loss of my mother when I was 12. I saw this tragedy, and the collateral damage it brought, as evidence of God's ambivalence and withdrawal from me.

"Maybe, when things 'pretty up' around here, then I will believe in a God who is good," I told myself as years passed.

But as my own daughters grew up, I realized I was going to need to deal with the ugliness I thought I had successfully walled off, in order to be healthy for them. So, like any educated woman, I searched for books about other women like myself. Astonishingly, at that time, I was only able to find one book, *Motherless Daughters* by Hope Edelman[1]. Aha! There is a name for me! I was getting somewhere!

But after I read that book, I wanted more. I wanted to know how this story ends. Both Edelman's loss and mine came about in the late 1970s when we were about the same age, the two of us. I needed to hear from someone who was no longer walking this difficult road of being a motherless mother, but from someone who had walked it already and had come to a deeply satisfying and assured place in her life, who could say to me, "It's going to be good. I promise."

No book for that?

Well, what do I do then?

Therapy is a good quest. But, for me, it ended up being just that. A quest that never seemed to end.

In therapy, I was prompted to keep asking the question I was already obsessively circling around - *why*?

What I found was the question of "Why?" led me into a perpetual circle of self-pity and self-focused thoughts that got me nowhere but deeper into a pit.

The turning point, for me, was in recognizing the hugely ferocious love I had for my daughters and the innate desire I had to be good to them. Where did I get that instinct?

It was here that the strangle hold of anxiety loosened as the lie that God doesn't love me was exposed. Of course He loves me. My standard for loving my own children was built into me by the One who *is* love. He is the Perfect Parent who allowed me to be a parent so that I could understand the depth of His love and goodness and the beauty He wants to give me.

Beauty doesn't reveal His Love. His Love reveals beauty.

The life I felt spoke of His ambivalence toward me turned out to be the classroom where I learned about His faithfulness to teach me all things, *in* all things. Through the experiences I will share with you, I learned the truth. God not only loves me and wants to be good to me, He pursues me. He not only wants to be present for me, He wants to be known. He is not silent and angry, He is speaking, in all things, of His loving ways.

I also discovered that you don't have to have lost a parent to have the spirit of an orphan. After all, in the most Biblical sense, we are all orphans, who have willfully walked away from our Father, to find the beauty and fulfillment we feel has been stolen or withheld from us. And as the Perfect Parent, God, skillfully does what so many of us have trouble doing. He waits for each of His children to be ready to hear Him, ready to willingly take His Hand, instead of forcing an involuntary and temporary attachment.

It is my hope, as I point out in my own stories, you will see that everything points to Him, and He speaks in all things, even in, especially in, most importantly in, your own story. God speaks. He wants to be heard. He wants to be seen and known.

God has related to me in a way that I can understand, which for me, has frequently been through movies and television. I think this is because I spent so much of my younger years perched in front of the television, watching reruns of old shows and movies that served to suspend the present I was so eager to escape. They remained constant and unchanging, despite the drastic change around me.

My daughters will corroborate that I frequently find God while I'm watching a movie with them and they are not always in the mood to hear how I see God in a particular plot line.

"Mommy, not *every* movie is about God!" they say, annoyed.

And I will come back swiftly and say, "Oh, but you see my dear little chickadees - *everything* points to God!"

The sooner you learn to look for Him, everywhere, the sooner you will learn to see Him - everywhere.

There will be times you get frustrated with me because I bounce around between understanding and enlightenment one moment, and fear and doubt the next. Bear with me. Like a delicious recipe that must marinate to become all that it can be, so too must wisdom and revelation be cured, steeped and incorporated into the mind and heart of the seeker.

I have spent many years trying to make sense of things, and if I can help anyone who thinks the emptiness they are feeling is because God has left, then I will feel like I have accomplished my purpose.

Part One

The Ashes

Chapter 1

Interrupted

Going to church was not on my schedule.

Yes, it was Sunday, but I had just dropped off my daughter at a dance intensive, being held in the massive basement of a church in New York City. I was planning to be a tourist on this beautiful summer day, not go to church.

The first thing on my "to-do" list was to hit Starbucks for my morning treat of a black half-caf. Oh, what I would've given to add a little half and half to my dull half-caf. But in an effort to get along with my middle–aged body, I chose to believe skipping the rich cream would make a difference. As I sat sipping, I felt an intense leading to go back to the church where I had just left Emmy and attend mass there. How long had it been since I had gone to a mass? Almost 20 years.

"Are you kidding me?" I thought, certain God and I had gotten our wires crossed on this one. "There is nothing there for me, Lord!"

Not only did I feel it would be an empty experience spiritually, I knew it would, ironically, fill me up in all the wrong ways, because there would be specific memories that would accompany me into that church to fill the void I would find there, if I dared to cross the threshold, and I wasn't willing to carry around those heavy memories today. It was not on my agenda.

I knew the Fat, Frizzy-haired girl would show up in the memories that would surely come. There were times when memories of this girl passed by with no ill-effect, but then, there were times that memories of her were the emotional equivalent of plunging into ice cold water. Thoughts of her had the power to take my breath away.

Delaying the church decision, I was watching a doggie drama unfold outside on the sidewalk as a woman became entangled by two rat-like dogs, crisscrossing their leashes in and around her ankles. My blank mind had given the Fat, Frizzy-haired girl access to me. From the vast hollow of my mind, she approached more quickly than I expected. She brought with her a rarely seen recollection:

> *It is a hot, sticky summer night in Indiana and I am looking all over the house for my mom. She is like a security blanket to me and I am never far from her. Both my sisters have friends sleeping over on this night, so I am particularly aware of a prolonged period of being left on my own.*
>
> *After looking all through the house for her, I push through the back door and find her sitting on the steps of our back porch. It is 1976 and she has just been diagnosed with breast cancer, which at this time, is certain death.*
>
> *"Hi baby," she spoke her usual greeting to me. She was holding her martini in one hand and a cigarette in the other.*

It's funny, the things you remember that don't really cause a ripple, until you stop to think about it a little more deeply - like why was my mom smoking a cigarette in this memory?

Hadn't she just been diagnosed with cancer?

Yep.

There will surely be many oddities that you, dear reader, will notice as I unpack my story for you. Many of them, like the cigarette alongside the cancer diagnosis, can be explained away with one sentence: It was the '70s. I'll do my best to acknowledge when these paradoxes occur, but there is a good chance I will miss some and leave you with your mouth hanging open. It's what makes some parts of this story darkly funny.

Not that cancer and cigarettes are funny, in any way, but the duality of sense and nonsense my family walked through in the '70s makes me shake my head as I recall this tragic memory.

Look, we either laugh about things like this or we cry. My upbringing taught me to avoid the tears, at all costs, and stick with laughing.

> *"What are you doing out here?" I ask her. Seeing my parents outside was just odd, especially in the backyard, which was really kid territory. I could have counted the number of times I had seen my mom sitting casually in our backyard. Her time "out back" was relegated only to when she mowed the lawn and weeded her massive flower gardens. But to just be sitting back here was strange. Like seeing people in a swimming pool fully clothed.*
>
> *I snugged up next to her, on the painted barn-red step, at the back of the magnificent house we lived in.*

> "*Do you know how many people commit suicide every day?*" *she asked, surely not expecting me to answer.*
>
> "*People kill themselves every day,*" *she continued.* "*They don't want to live.*"
>
> *Where was she going with this? I knew she had cancer, but I had not understood what it meant for her. For us. I was perplexed by this conversation. I was only about 10 years old, and this was not making sense to me.*
>
> *I was still hung up on the oddity of finding her in such an unusual place, almost as if she had been hiding, but from whom? Why was she talking about suicide?*
>
> "*I want to live!*" *her voice quivered.*
>
> "*What do you mean?*" *I looked up at her and asked, scared to hear her words.*

As a child, you really don't think your parents are ever going to die, especially not your mom. I had never considered this possibility. This was my mom. Moms don't die. They live on and are there for you, until you are a grown up and you can bear, even expect, the loss. They love you more than anyone else ever could or ever will. They stay.

They don't go away and leave you with an alcoholic father who has no idea who these three girls are who have his last name. They don't die and leave you with a grandmother who is quietly being led away by dementia, but nobody knows or recognizes because it is only 1970-something and the average person doesn't really know about Alzheimer's yet.

They don't die. They don't leave. But she did.

Forcefully, purposefully, heaving this memory off, I bring myself back to the core matter at hand: "To go or not to go to church today".

The tugging for me to go to church I could accommodate, just not *that* church. You see, I was raised in this particular denomination and, in my adulthood, had grown to have great disdain for that upbringing. It was all tied up with my judgement of the poor job my parents did of being parents and the anger I had at my childhood God for the poor job He did of being God.

God had been absent for us all those desperate years we sought Him in church. This delineation soothed me and offered explanation as to why prayers for my mom to live had never been answered.

"I had been looking for Him in the wrong place," I deduced. "He hadn't been there, in our church, that's why He never answered me."

This explanation eventually freed me to pursue the loving God I heard about. It'd been almost 20 years since I encountered and began walking with this loving, caring God. Knowing Him had changed me, changed the way I regarded the sad assumption that He had let me down. I forgave His silence because I had surmised He hadn't been there. It was a simple and necessary thread I had to stitch into our relationship because it was the only way to account for His inactivity during those years.

So yes, I would love to go to church and worship my loving, good God today. But not there. Had to be a mistake. I pulled out my phone to look for a "safe" church that would be more welcoming and familiar to me at this point in my life. Laziness, however, got the best of me and I was unwilling to walk the 30 minutes to get to a "friendlier" church, so, I gave in.

I was practiced at questioning where God wanted me to go and equally practiced at finally giving in, following God where He led me, always being blessed through His unusual requests. "There must be a reason You want me to go."

Slowly gathering my belongings and my courage, I took one last sip of the coffee and tossed it in the trash on the way out the door. It felt strange and intimidating to be going back to the church that I felt had let me down all those years.

Climbing the impressive, concrete steps of the cathedral, I was virtually alone, indicating to me that I was either really early or really late. I didn't like either possibility. Once inside the stately doors, it appeared I was early. The church was so enormous; it would take quite a crowd to make it look anything close to well-attended. This was a relief to me; I wouldn't be so conspicuous in a church this size.

Immediately, I notice the sweet, smoky incense that must have been burned earlier. Normally, this smell, in this setting, would bring a haunting sadness with it, a reminder of the Fat, Frizzy-haired girl at a tragic, premature funeral.

But today? Today the fragrance is welcome. It doesn't cast my spirit down; it ignites unexpected sentiment. I even find myself hoping to see the priest waving the decanter that will send out more of the musky aroma.

The vast quiet in the historic sanctuary is alive and

every sound is magnified. Putting one foot in front of the other, aware of each footfall as it catapults off the towering, arched ceiling, this beautiful echo holds reverence for me today, the way a glass holds water, and I am shocked at how thirsty I am for it. I drink it in.

It is undeniable; I'm *excited* to be here.

The nervousness I felt before has been converted to eagerness. I am anticipating the ceremony now, longing to be comforted by the familiarity of the mass, for its acquaintanceship to lay on me like a treasured quilt. Like a dancer, whose muscles remember the steps of a dance she hasn't performed in years, I remember to genuflect and make the sign of the cross before I edge into the long, wooden pew. The groan and slight movement of the creaky bench as I sit is like putting on a well-fitting leather glove.

Ceremoniously, the priest and the folks who have volunteered to serve for mass make their way down the aisle leading to the altar. It strikes me as funny how the woman in this official procession, who is carrying the Bible over her head, also has her purse slung across her body, the "urban liturgical look", I think, amusing myself.

Accompanied by a piano and flute, the cantor begins singing, but in this massive church, anything less than the pipe organ causes him to sound a capella. Even better, as far as I'm concerned. I eagerly and loudly sing the opening with him. Ah, now he holds up his hands and my pew mates sing too. I had forgotten to wait for this prompting from him that signals when the congregation is invited to sing along. Will they think I'm weird for singing out of turn? Will they think I don't know the deal here? I don't even care.

Here I am embracing the rituals I had all but forgotten about. Understanding, today, the comfort coming from them. The smells, the sounds, the music, they are a salve to my soul that I didn't know I needed. The ceremony that used to get me fidgeting in my seat now has me glued there.

And so it goes. We sing the alleluias and hosannas. I am an adult, with the gift of a family of my own now. A gift I recognize coming from the God I grew up fearing, in a church just like this one.

I am not the Fat, Frizzy-haired, 12-year-old girl with the tremendous injury of losing her momma to the cancer that ate its way past her breast and into her lungs and liver, dreadfully and heinously consuming her. The back porch memory this morning was just that. A passing memory that had been, for the most part, disarmed already, by the same God who nudged me to attend mass this morning.

And here, right here, is where I hear, deep within, "I was there." The warmth of understanding gently cascading, settling peacefully, beautifully, coating me from the inside out.

"I was there."

He had brought me here to show me another piece of the puzzle He'd been putting together for me ever since I agreed to listen. Coming to this church today had been a gift. He was telling me He'd been there with me, even before the tragedy, in the very place, the church, where I had grown to resent and distrust Him.

"I was there."

What do you do when such power rushes over you? Like a forceful wave, that one line, swallowed up and washed away much of the confusion and sadness regarding this place that I'd smuggled in with me.

And it is here that I experience my "movie moment", the present moment being blurred out, the memories flooding in, insistent on my acknowledging them.

Chapter 2
It Was The '70s

Not all my memories this morning hold such gravity. I am met by PC (pre-cancer) memories, of when we were just a typical middle-class '70s family, doing typical middle-class '70s things, when life wasn't so heavy.

Maybe I should explain. My personal experience and interpretation is that the '70s were a strange decade. Let me start by saying that my own parents don't define a generation of parents. But my parents certainly defined my world. Looking back, I can get some clarity on their behalf when I examine the history of the era. Global and social events leading up to the tumultuous '70s created a perfect storm of extremes that led to the counterculture that emerged for some.

My folks had been children during the depression and World War II. Kids raised during this economically disastrous and uncertain time were not chased around by parents making sure they were happy and whole. Their own parents were in a monumental battle to hang onto their homes, their life savings, their jobs and to put some meager amount of food on the table. Raising emotionally healthy children was not the goal. They were just trying to make it through the day. I think it was this aspect of my parents' history that gave them the basis for their bare bones parenting style.

Layer on top of that my parents' experience of being young adults in the iconic, gold standard of the "good old days" that was the 1950's. An exuberant nation celebrated an economic, post-war boom and the traditional values of the country were held in high regard. But the country was groaning under the heaviness of pre-civil rights racism, the fear of far-off tyranny encroaching our shores, and a restlessness for change among young people.

The once honored tenets my parents grew up with were radically rejected in the social and political chaos of the 1960s, leaving some young adults in moral free fall. The boundaries, the discipline and strictness they encountered as youngsters were scorned by the generation born after them. I think there were people my parents' age who felt pressure to disavow their own sense of what was good and right. The world they had known as children melted away as life became about dissatisfaction with, and rejection of, the status quo.

They must've had a hard time knowing where they fit, sandwiched between old world values for the greater good and new world hedonism that was self-focused.

I believe this is what gave birth to my '70's parents. They carried with them the heavy, pessimistic impressions made during their early lives of barely surviving economically and emotionally to the increasingly popular mantra of "What about me?" that came when the old guard was overthrown during the turbulent Civil Rights movement and Vietnam war.

One thing that remained from the old guard for my folks, however, was the dismal outlook that you just had to make it through the day. Five o'clock was a daily goal for Bart and Francie Murphy, and certainly for many of the adults I encountered in the confines of our little world. When the big hand was on the twelve and the little hand was on the five, the heaviness they carried was surrendered as the martini passed over their lips. They would not have to pick up their burdens again until the next morning when, through a pounding headache and blood-shot eyes, they set their sights on the renewed goal of making it to the next "happy" hour.

Parenting collided with the conviction, "It's my turn for things to be about me!" And voila! My '70's parents emerged. As a child in this dichotomous era, it is only in looking back that I wonder, "What were they thinking?!" At the time, however, it was just how we lived. My sisters and I have spent a lot of hours amused and bewildered and sometimes, horrified, over the years as we recall some of the choices they made, those '70's parents of ours.

For example, we didn't think it odd, at the time, that we were sent home with the cleaning lady from the hotel where we were vacationing in Florida, so my parents could party all night without the boundaries imposed on them by their children. All three of us sisters have very vivid memories of sharing the full-sized bed at the stranger's house that night, chanting "bourbon and water, bourbon and water" until we lulled ourselves to sleep. This was not odd or dangerous. It was just the '70s!

Back in those days, in my little town, I went to church, but hadn't known to look for a loving God while I was sitting with the congregation. I endured innumerable, boring masses where I came to believe God was angry at me and that my parents, too, were typically angry at us.

I was scolded in church and tried to get my sisters

scolded, as well. I have vivid memories of goosing my sister on the way up to communion, hoping to make her "mess up" somehow and incur the wrath of my father.

My sister, Kellie, was my Irish twin, which meant there was less than a year between us. Eleven months, to be exact. Kellie and I shared the desire to avoid church. We'd get up early on Sunday mornings to hide behind the coats in the abnormally large walk-in coat closet in our stately home. This is the very closet my dad made me eat my dinner in when I had the nerve to eat too slowly. And everyone's okay with this? Come on! It wasn't child abuse. It was the '70s! To this day, I lament that punishment as I chow down my food before anyone has had time to pick up their fork.

Anyway, the theory behind our Sunday morning hide and seek was that if, by chance, everyone was awake in time to go to mass, they wouldn't be able to find Kellie and I, hiding behind the rows of coats, and the mission would be scrapped. The odds were in our favor. Usually my mom and dad would be hung over from our night out at the All You Can Eat Fish Fry the night before.

We didn't think anything of being driven home from the fish fry in the darkness of the early, early morning. So very proud of his Irish heritage and all that title embodied, Bart Murphy considered it his duty to be the life of the party and the last to leave it. That left a lot of time for cocktails. Once everyone was gone, no other cars left in the parking lot, we were corralled for the drunken drive home.

What? You didn't do this?

You didn't watch your dad put the car in drive-except, not really, because his hand slipped off the gearshift? He went through the motions of driving home, as if in a simulator, pretending to maneuver through the parking lot, except that he wasn't maneuvering anywhere because, remember, the car was still in park.

My mom, you ask? She was on the pretend ride home as well.

"Bart, the car's not in gear," she eventually prompted. When we finally made it home, she was the one who put me to bed.

"Sweet dreams, Bridgie," she called back to me on her way out of my room. Then BAM! She walked right into the wall.

I mention all of this to underscore that the chances of them getting up in time for church were slim on most weekends. Thanks to their party habits, we really weren't burdened with going to church all that much. When we did go, it was rare for daddy to join us.

"Let your father sleep," my mom would instruct us, which was fine with my sisters and me.

Daddy was a scary guy, so we were happy to let him sleep and put off his appearance for a few more hours. But when daddy did go to church with us?

Well, then, there was often a trip to the church basement for chocolate milk and donuts with pink frosting. There in the basement, with the moms in their vogue clothes and the coiffured hairstyles they went to the salon once a week for, the priests would mingle among us without the formality of the adorned frock they wore during the mass. Dressed in "basement attire" - black pants, a short-sleeved black shirt with the white tab collar across his neck, our Monsignor would swing the smaller kids around and pretend to magically pull pennies out of their ears.

"How about if we go to out for breakfast?" my dad would propose from time to time, if he was in a good mood. Let me say that back then, people didn't go out to eat as frequently as we do now. It was a real treat to be taken out.

Now, we had two choices for breakfast in town. There was Sammy's and the Golden Waffle. As lively as Sammy's was, we preferred the Golden Waffle, because it was in the mall and, being Sunday, the mall wasn't open. However, if you were lucky enough to go to the GW, you were granted "special access" to the empty shopping center via the secret entrance, open only for Golden Waffle patrons.

My, we have memories from the Golden Waffle, the best one about my oldest sister, Marie, who was in middle school at the time. Mind you, this trip to the GW became very uncool post- 5th grade, so it was no treat for her.

Get the whole vision of Marie on this day. Granny glasses, braces, the home perm my mom gave her that resulted in a small, tight afro, suede chukka boots - which weren't all that fashionable in our small town, a plaid maxi coat, and clothes which belonged to my mom.

Marie had pitched a fit that morning, "I don't have anything to wear!!" she'd complained angrily.

Screaming, "I don't have anything to wear!!!" didn't mean you would be treated to a shopping spree after church because, poor you, you little orphan child, you have nothing to wear.

No. It meant you would be given something ridiculous to wear and proudly paraded through the Golden Waffle in your mom's clothes because you boldly and unwisely had a temper tantrum to get out of going to church.

You see, in this bygone era, parents frequently used humiliation to teach us a good lesson. It's not like now, when we "helicopter parents" do our best to rescue our children from moments that might cause deep humiliation. Back then, humiliation was employed as a teaching tool. Something to make the most of. It was the reason we were taken out for breakfast on that aqqqw day, to make Marie's lesson all that more powerful!

Like those excursions after church, I remember other happy, light-hearted times before my mom got sick.

There were family vacations to exotic places like Myrtle Beach, South Carolina, THE destination for a hip family at the time.

We drove the 15 plus hours to South Carolina, because families of five didn't fly back then.

"Bring everything out to the car," my dad ordered, while my mom was inside scouring the kitchen sink. "I can't stand to come home to a dirty house," she'd say, and this would be engrained in me as an adult.

Leaning on the sleek Impala, the trunk open, daddy surveyed the belongings we brought out. Cigarette in hand, and one behind his ear, he haphazardly jammed the suitcases, sleeping bags, pillows and bags of food into the car. We girls were crammed into the back seat, free to fly around, because nobody wore those pesky seatbelts at the time. My assigned seat was in the middle, precariously balanced on the luggage and sleeping bags that hadn't fit into the trunk. And off we went, to cruise the open road.

"Stop touching me!" I quietly growled at Kellie, who inevitably took up more than her allotted space in the backseat.

"If you don't stop bickering, I'm going to pull this car over!" daddy shot back.

And he did pull the car over.

He lined us up along the side of the car, like criminals along a police car about to be frisked while he made the dreaded grab for his belt.

"Ffffffffffftttt" it hissed as it was unleashed from the loops that held it in place.

Down the line, he spanked us along the side of the road for all to see, without fear of being reported to Child Protective Services. We packed ourselves back into the car, and all was quiet again, until Kellie had the guts to overstep her boundaries again.

Almost all my family memories are peppered with disciplinary intercessions, proving that even if we were on vacation, Daddy's watchful eye was always roving.

My mom was the soft touch. She found out there was a state park along our route and she packed a picnic lunch for us to enjoy. Hours into our trip, with the excitement and anticipation building for the last few hours about the picnic, we finally arrived and unloaded the smorgasbord. It was all fun, until, in a moment of unbridled pleasure, Kellie made a Grave Error.

"This is how Hoss eats!" Kellie informed us, referring to the big, fat, beast of a brother on the popular television show, Bonanza. Holding a chicken leg up to her mouth, her arm cranked out to the side, Kellie took a huge bite and pulled the drumstick away, the meat dangling from her mouth. Bad manners were not her only Unforgivable Offense. She then hurled the chicken leg behind her, into the grass. Polluting - her second offense - was too much for my dad to sit idly by and watch.

"You think that's funny?" Daddy snarled at her.

"No, sir," Kellie conceded meekly, in the "Ma'am and Sir-ese" with which my father was adamant we address my mother and him.

"You're really not going to think it's funny when you're picking up all the trash in the park after lunch."

Well, Kellie may not have thought it was funny, but Marie and I secretly knew it was. Nothing better than seeing your sister "get it", especially since she'd had the audacity to continue to cross the backseat boundary lines all morning. Maybe this would humble her a little and settle her down.

Only one other thing sticks out in my mind about this vacation, which was how we all got criminally sunburned, to the point of having blisters and chills and being incapacitated each night. I am just taking a stab here, but I don't think sunscreen was widely used or available. If it was, it was news to us fair-skinned, Irish girls. Mommy sprayed us down each night with Solarcaine and dutifully took precautions the next day by making us wear our souvenir, Myrtle Beach t-shirts in the pool. This was a great '70's remedy for a sunburn that worked like a charm. The wet t-shirt stuck to and pulled away the crisp, bubbling skin, leaving a forever scar, a souvenir of the family vacation.

We had quite a privileged life, by all standards of the time. There were regular family vacations and even a lake cottage. Our historic, grand home was somewhat of a modern, middle class Gatsby-style party house. My mom and dad were very outgoing and loved to entertain. It was a time when average, everyday people got gussied up, sort of red-carpet style, and went to dinner parties at each other's houses. Now, this isn't like the dinner parties I have now, where friends volunteer to bring a dish and the kids are invited to come along.

The memo pad with all of Mommy's notes, like the guest list and the menu, would be laying around the kitchen for weeks. Silver would be polished, and my mom would make herself a new evening gown for the gala. Mommy was successful at every role she took on, including fashion designer and seamstress, so her gowns were exquisite.

One gown I remember her making upstairs in her "sewing room," just a large closet she converted, was a silver and black sparkly getup that made her look like a movie star. When she went down the grand staircase that night to welcome the first guests, the dog hitched a ride on the train of her dress and bumped down each step behind her, refusing to move. We girls watched from the open hallway upstairs, because we were not allowed to be around during these grand parties.

Sometimes, Mommy hired a babysitter to stay upstairs with us while the grown-ups had first a cocktail hour and then a gourmet meal at the richly-set table in the formal dining room. As we got older, Mary Tyler Moore, Carol Burnett and Bob Newhart were entrusted to "babysit" us, the tray of tea sandwiches delivered earlier by my decked-out momma, who loved her girls and loved entertaining and was the life of the party. Everyone loved her. And everyone loved her parties.

The guest list ranged from neighbors to the doctors that my dad called on in his job as a pharmaceutical salesman. My two sisters and I would lean over the railing, as far as we safely could, with high hopes of catching a glimpse of something below. Shirley Bassey or Neil Diamond played on the giant, furniture-style, console stereo in the hallway. We could hear laughing and see bits of ladies' gowns, but we never got much more than that.

As the festivities wore on, some of the guests would come up to "check on us." This was always after the party had been going on for a few hours, so our visitors would undoubtedly be a little tipsy or completely smashed and slurring their words. They meant well. I have no idea how these party guests got home or if there was a designated driver, but I must err on the side of assuming there were some tipsy drivers dispersed on the road as the parties wound down. But people didn't think about those things in the '70s.

There didn't have to be an official party for people to gather at our house. My mom was so much fun to be around and my dad so famous for his surly, racy sense of humor, if a party wasn't planned, on any given night, there might be a spontaneous gathering on our expansive front porch that lasted well into the night. Bart and Francie were living the dream.

Yes, there were happy memories growing up. I know it may sound funny to consider roadside beatings, sun poisoning and sequestration as happy memories, but this was part and parcel of growing up in that era. These were normal events in our "normal," '70s family.

But there was a dark side to our private life. Not all the moments resulted in fun memories. Many of them erupted into out of control, alcohol-fueled drama, bordering precariously on potential crime scenes.

I remember one night; violence took hold while we were at our lake cottage. I use the term "cottage" generously. It was really a one-room cabin with a front and back porch, the kitchen being jammed into the front porch, an after-market 'toilet shack" tacked onto the side for good measure. Yes, I could've said bathroom, but that word doesn't pinpoint accurately the state of the facilities quite the way toilet shack does.

Anyway, Kellie and I were there with my mom and dad, who had begun their happy hour a little early-to accommodate a date with our neighbors at the lake, whom they were going to play cards with later that evening. So, with that in mind, Bart and Francie sat down in the one room cabin at the tank of a dining room table. The table looked like it would've graced the quarters of a captain at sea. It was massive. It still donned the original, perpetually sticky, vinyl tablecloth that had been draped over it before we were the proud owners, and was absolutely, hopelessly stuck to the table forevermore.

Sipping their martinis, engaging in what seemed to be small talk, I tuned in when I noticed them getting loud. It seems my mom, who was a stay-at-home mom back then, just as it was going out of style, mentioned how it upset her that she worked to make our home look so beautiful and my dad's boxes of drug samples, which he received almost daily because of his job, were always in the grand foyer, clogging up the view.

Francie Murphy was an incredible homemaker. Our home had been a diamond in the rough when she got hold of it. She made the run-down, over-sized house a beautiful home (think Mary Bailey from *It's a Wonderful Life* [2]here!). It was a full-time job. And so, after a few sips of gin, she got a little outspoken about how she wished my dad would put the "corrugated accessories" that came with his job into the basement. Can you blame her? Well, Daddy became enraged. It was the only time I ever witnessed him physically attack her, and it was terrifying.

He sneered at her, aggressively flicking his cigarette onto the worn carpet. He got in her face and clearly provoked her with whatever he was saying. Things escalated quickly, and the two were wrestling between their thrown-back chairs. Daddy's hands wrapped around Mommy's neck, her arms flailing, scratching at him, trying to defend herself from her attacker, her husband.

Kellie and I tried pulling my dad away. He wasn't budging. Mommy continued to struggle as we beat impotently at daddy's legs. We thought he was going to kill her.

The next thing I remember is my dad on the front porch, the "kitchen," wiping the scratches on his face with a cloth. My mom had taken refuge in the toilet shack and I could hear her sobbing. I recall standing in the kitchen thinking: "This is going to change everything. Finally."

You see, Bart and Francie and their happy hours were a volatile mix and I remember several frightening episodes, followed by my mom creeping into my room to comfort my stifled weeping after daddy had verbally abused me or her or both of us.

"Tomorrow, I'm going to call a lawyer and find out about a divorce," she offered more than once. It soothed me. I hated my dad. I was afraid of him. Sober, he was mean-spirited. But when he drank, he was intimidating and abusive. Usually not physically, but he used the imminent threat of it. On this night at the lake, he pulled it out and wielded it as the weapon he had always kept on reserve.

I think my mom thought this would finally cause things to change as well. There's only so much pressure that can build up without an eventual eruption. Mommy seemed to be in the midst of the assuredness that it was time to do something about the way we lived.

She emerged from the bathroom, gulping back sobs. Her face deeply scratched, red and blotchy, she could hardly breathe. Her whole body hiccupped as she tried to keep in the tears that had waited so long to be released. She wouldn't look at Kellie or me-wouldn't reassure us that everything was okay. Neither of them spoke. It was quiet and eerie.

To keep up appearances, we went to the neighbors', as scheduled. My mom played cards and pretended that everything was normal. Because that was the only choice she had in 1970-something. She had no job, no prospects of a job, and three daughters. Divorce, back then, would mean the end of the financial and social advantage she enjoyed as Mrs. Murphy, as well as swift religious ex-communication. She was trapped.

Accompanying them to the neighbors' house, Kellie and I wrapped ourselves loyally and desperately around the legs of the chair my mom sat in, laying our heads on her legs from time to time while she patted our heads, sipped another martini, anted up her chips, and continued that dreadful gasping for breath that comes when your heart needs to keep weeping but your brain tells you to shut up.

It wasn't until I was in the 5th grade that I can put the first blip of my mom's illness into sequence.

The Thing That Would Forever Shape My Life.

This was shortly before the Back Porch Meeting I mentioned earlier.

I don't know exactly how the whole process started for her or how she discovered the lump in her breast, but for me, it started when she was going to have a biopsy.

I didn't understand what this meant. I was mostly scared of her dying in surgery.

I didn't know about cancer and medical procedures, but I had grown up watching Medical Center [3] and Marcus Welby, and I knew that sometimes, people didn't make it!

"How about if I have your Daddy call you when I get out of surgery? Would that make you feel better?" my mom suggested.

My dad had been thoroughly disgusted by this arrangement, "You spoil these kids," he had chided my mother.

The next day, sitting at the emerald green picnic tables in the art room at school, wearing my cool Raggedy

Ann smock, the school secretary came in and whispered in my ear.

"Your mom is out of surgery and she's okay."

To my mind, that meant that, well, my mom was okay.

But to the more sophisticated, grown up mind, this announcement only meant she'd made it through the biopsy alive. It said nothing about what was discovered in the biopsy.

This was just the beginning of It, the monstrous journey that would seize and compel us into a decades-long typhoon. Only we didn't know that then. Mercifully.

In keeping with their bizarre parenting choices, my mom and dad brought Kellie and me to the hospital with them when they went to get the biopsy results. However, before you judge them too harshly, please understand they didn't actually bring us *in* to the hospital, to be subjected to what could be a very emotional reaction to a possible life changing diagnosis. Come on! What do you think they were? Stupid?

No. They left us locked in the car in the parking garage.

Now, I am only piecing this all together as an adult. At the time, I had no idea the weightiness and importance of why we were locked in the car. It wasn't like they said to us, in a tender, Hallmark moment, "Girls, we are going to the hospital to see if Mommy is sick. This could either be really good and she'll be fine, or, it could be really bad and she could die."

No, not like that at all.

It was probably more like, "Wait here and don't touch

anything." For the generation who raised their families in this unique decade, and in the decades previous, children were to be seen and not heard.

In what must've taken monumental repose or unbelievable ignorance, my mom tapped on the car window and made a funny face at us when they finally returned, acting as if nothing was wrong. We had no idea the severity of what was about to unfold and truthfully, I am guessing my mom didn't either. I'm assuming the conversation with the doctor had gone something like this:

"Mrs. Murphy, you have a malignancy in your breast."

"Will I have to have a mastectomy?" my mother would've said, in a panic at the thought of losing the coveted body part.

"No, of course not. We'll just barely remove the lump. You'll be fine!"

"Okay, PHEW!"

Because, from what I can retrace, my mom's biggest concern was that she would have to have breast removed. If she had been promised that she could keep her esteemed woman part, she would've been good with that. It wasn't that she was shallow, but most women back then regarded things differently.

Years before, she should've had a hysterectomy, but opted, instead, for a D and C. My question now, as a woman is, "Why do you want to hang onto that uterus? You already used it. You really don't need it anymore."

But, this is back before hormone replacement and breast reconstruction and back before women felt they could be okay on their own. I think my mom must have felt like she'd have been less of a woman for my father, and, if that were the case, one thing could lead to another. Maybe he would have an affair with a "real woman" who had all her lady parts. I'm not certain this is what her reasoning was, but it's a construct that has offered me a valid explanation as to why she would have held onto those parts that were, one by one, betraying her.

After leaving the hospital that day, we went to my grandmother's house, where my mom explained to her mother what was happening. They cried. I didn't understand. It was decided grandma would come stay at our house while my mom underwent the treatment for breast cancer, which for her was a short round of hitting her upper body with radiation and narrowly pulling out the lump from the breast (seems they didn't worry about clean margins) my mother was so adamant about not losing.

I honestly can't remember the true course of things. So many stages and tests to this whole diagnosis and treatment. In the end, months later, there was great rejoicing and a naïve belief, by all involved, that Francie Murphy had beat the cancer. We were free to go on with our lives!

Chapter 3
Mean Grandma Betty

I was at school in the rough part of town the year my mom received her clean bill of health.

Certain mysterious zoning things had taken place and I was sentenced to one year, 6th grade, in the bad section of town. After that one year, I would be allowed to join the rest of my neighborhood friends, who had already proceeded directly to the Nice School to start their middle school journey.

It wasn't like I had a choice. I acquiesced and went to the rough school with the kids who had not known all the privilege that I had. It was just for one year. But, because the lives of the kids at this school were so different than mine, and with the huge impact it had on my social standing ever after, it may as well have been miles away for years and years.

This was a rough crowd of kids. They probably had never even been in the secret passageway to the Golden Waffle! Their idea of recreation was to smoke cigarettes in the parking lot after school and beat up little nit wits that naively entered the scene late, like me.

I was a chubby, wire-haired little girl at the time. After all, the only dieting we knew of was to not eat too many Ding Dongs before dinner and the only hair product we had was mayonnaise which did nothing to tame the advent of coarse hair that corrupted my scalp once puberty began. Not only was I a round little plug of a thing with a less than ideal head of hair, I also had a lisp. It caught the attention of my homeroom teacher who shuffled me into speech therapy once a week. Now, I don't know if no one picked up on the lisp prior to this, but how could they have missed it? Or, maybe a speech therapist in school was a new-fangled thing. But it seems to me that 6th grade was a little late in the game to be starting to attack this problem.

At any rate, I, along with a few other kids, sat in a sectioned-off corner of an office once a week and worked with Miss Riggs, the speech therapist, whose very name was a cruel joke to the kid with a speech impediment!

Miss Riggs instructed me to clench my teeth together hard and keep my tongue glued to the inside of my bottom teeth and say, "sssssssssssssssssssss" over and over until I finally graduated to saying "sssssss-tar" and "ssssss-nake".

At the end of the few weeks we were together, there was a graduation ceremony. Sitting at the table with my mom, who had received a special invitation to attend this bright, shining moment in my passing through adolescence, I was nailing every flash card Miss Riggs could throw at me.

"Missssssss Riggsssssss, I ssssssssee a sssssssstar," I finally got out through my locked jaw. I could tell by her slight nod; Miss Riggs approved of my progress and saw it for what it was-a miraculous breakthrough!

But my mom? Well, she wasn't so impressed with the ground-breaking work Miss Riggs and I had been doing. She sat in the miniature, student-sized chair that had been provided, her purse on her lap and her hands clasped tightly over the handle, looking down, so as not to let me see her face. I didn't have to see her face to know what she was thinking. Although I couldn't hear it, the fact that her whole body was shaking told me she was laughing-laughing-at this fine accomplishment of mine.

She had a sense of humor, my mom. The sight of her daughter with lockjaw, painfully pushing out the famous "Miss Riggs I see a _____" became a staple for making us laugh.

Mommy was involved with a lot of community projects and charities. Once she took my friend and me to the high school basketball game and afterwards, she sent us off to collect all the red and white, waxed, Coca-Cola cups that we could rescue from the trash and under the bleachers because, somehow, these were involved in her latest fundraiser. That is the last night I remember as a carefree kid.

Sometime after that, the cancer came back.

That summer, when I was 12 and would be rejoining my former classmates at the Nice School in the coming fall, my mom was in the hospital the whole summer getting chemotherapy. The whole summer. Daddy went to work every day and then drove the hour to the hospital every night to be with her. Since the edict was for us to be seen and not heard, we were never permitted, much less invited, to go see her.

"How are the kids doing?" you would think someone would've asked. But not back then. At least, not in our world. Even though it was not all that long ago, parenting styles have changed beyond recognition. What was thought of, by some, as appropriate parenting back then could now be regarded as negligent at best, abusive at worst.

No one gave the three daughters a second thought. To their minds, this was none of our business. All eyes and resources were focused on my mom and dad. Do I sound bitter? Not bitter. Just perplexed. But I know with certainty that this aspect of my childhood, this intense loneliness and feeling left behind, had more influence on my own parenting choices than anything else. I would never allow my children to think they didn't matter or their circumstances were not important.

During this long summer, we stayed home with Mean Grandma Betty, or MGB, that's what I called her. Or at least, I stayed home with her. Marie was well into her teen years and had a job and a life of her own at that point, so she wasn't home much. Kellie, too, had friends to lean on that summer and could escape the house. Which left me profoundly alone.

With a new school on the horizon, I knew I had to spend that summer getting reconnected with old friends, to avoid the unspeakable trauma of Standing Alone on that first day at the Nice School, waiting for the bell to ring. I already felt like a stranger to those girls I had grown up with, simply from that one year of separation. So, I had work to do to get back "in"!

And that, not so much my mother, was initially the focus of that summer for me, because I didn't understand the implications of her situation.

A summer with Betty was not ideal. Born into a wealthy family in 1906, Grandma had lived a lavish life, coming of age in the Flapper Era. There are early pictures of her looking beautiful with heavy lipstick and bobbed hair hidden under a hat, stealing a drink from a flask she and her girlfriends were sharing, their long fur coats and fancy dresses marking them as privileged and carefree.

Enter Henry, a very handsome young fellow who did not share her sophisticated background or family stature. This simply would not do. Grandma's wealthy family told Betty that if she continued to carouse with this young hooligan, there would be consequences. So, she stopped carousing with Henry, and married him, instead. Her family disowned her. She was cut off from her parents, her siblings, their money and their life of ease.

To be fair, the privileged lifestyle wouldn't be around much longer for anyone. By the time Betty and Henry got married and had children, the stock market had crashed and tough times fell upon most everyone, whether they had been shunned by their wealthy families or not.

They had first one daughter and then my mother, Francie. Mommy was born in 1933 and reaped all the "benefits" of being born at such an unfortunate time in history. She was a sickly child, even relegated to bed for an entire year, because she had a heart condition. She also had extreme eczema and related stories of being teased mercilessly by students and mistreated by teachers who gave her the "Rudolph treatment". "No red, scaly- handed kid is gonna join in our reindeer games, right kid?"

Still, Mommy's family fared better than most. Grandpa was employed as a policeman and walked a beat in their quaint New England town. They lived three houses back from the beach, and Mommy told how she'd been caught in a riptide when she was young. She grew into an adult who was mortally afraid of water.

The debonair Henry eventually enlisted in the army when WWII started and was promptly shipped off overseas, leaving Grandma home with little money and no plan for security. It must've been difficult, as a single mom, to raise two kids during this uncertain era. Such were the times. There were many, many families suddenly headed by single mothers, with husbands and fathers fighting for freedom an ocean away.

After the war, my grandfather was one of the lucky ones who returned home, physically intact, but perhaps not so much emotionally. He moved the family from their beloved home in New England to the Midwest, where he secured a factory job with the promise of good money. He had been a devoted soldier, but once he returned home, he didn't remain devoted to my grandmother. Fidelity, it seems, lost its importance to him after the war. Once they were settled, Betty also got a factory job. Worn out from his wandering ways, she divorced Henry swiftly after she saved some money.

My mom and her sister had a few rowdy years as they came of age. I heard lots of stories about friends, parties, sneaking out and climbing in the house through the bedroom window. And there were road trips. Lots of road trips. Sometimes, Grandma even joined them on their girl adventures. They all longed to be back in New England and took many trips back east.

When my aunt gave birth to my cousin, things calmed down a little. Betty deeply loved and nurtured this baby. Because my aunt had to work, and Grandma was retired, she got to spend a lot of time with my cousin. They had a beautiful relationship. My cousin called her "Granny Bear."

I mention this because Betty was never that nice, squishy and loveable woman for me, especially the second time, when Mommy's cancer came back, and MGB came to stay with us again, temporarily...wink wink.

Looking back on Grandma's life, from my adult perspective, I see she had already trudged through a difficult life. Disowned by her family, raising children during first the Depression and then a war, an unfaithful husband and a marriage that ended in divorce, she had already raised two generations of children. She had to have been tired and looking forward to some rest and the prosperity of her pension when along came three more girls who needed tending.

And let's not forget the reason these three children needed tending. Her own youngest daughter, her obvious favorite, was ill again, perhaps terminally. So, to be fair, Grandma headed into this task strictly out of obligation, with the coat of sorrow and fear wrapped tightly around her. It wasn't like coming to visit the grandkids and then going home. She was coming to take care of her daughter, though it was not known then how bad this was going to get.

The fateful summer when Mommy was hospitalized and Daddy was ragged from days upon days of working, worrying and commuting back and forth to the hospital, and as we girls all tried desperately to hold our places in our fragile, adolescent worlds, Mean Grandma Betty was a Depression-era, mildly abusive, drill sergeant.

The typical daily routine was for MGB to wake Kellie

and I up by 7:00 A.M., calling out and deploring our laziness.

"Get up!" she'd order cantankerously. "You girls aren't going to sleep all day."

"Good morning, Grandma," we sometimes offered.

"What's good about it?" she faithfully snapped back. Okay, so that's how it's gonna be today.

There were chores to be done and no time for pleasantries! The lawn had to be tended. The massive peony garden, my mother's pride and joy, had to be waded into and weeded, along with her rose garden. The ever-popular plastic, green AstroTurf that made its way onto the now quiet Party Porch had to be cleaned by Kellie and I, on hands and knees, picking up minute bits of debris, Joan-Crawford-style. What's wrong with a broom or a vacuum you might ask? It didn't pass the standards of MGB. She wanted it done the "right way." She didn't trust vacuum cleaners or other modern marvels. She had disdain for all things new and "innovative."

I dreaded the mornings, not to mention the emptiness of the day that waited for me once our tasks were complete. I didn't begrudge the chore doing. I just didn't agree with the aggressive and contemptuous way she went about assigning them. Nor did I appreciate the fact that we had to carry them out as if we were living on the prairie during the Dust Bowl, with no modern technology to assist us.

And like any dutiful sister who will never let a fear go unexploited, Kellie capitalized on the angst centered around our daily revelry. One day, she wrestled a pair of tan panty hose over her head and hovered over my face until I woke up. I opened my eyes to the smashed, grotesque, silent face. This was her way of lightening the mood we knew would slam into the room as soon as MGB stormed in. Ah! The fun you can have amid dysfunction.

There were daily misfortunes that came from being under MGB's tutelage. Poor Kellie, when she got her period for the first time, without the presence of a loving and compassionate mother around, was at the mercy of MGB who didn't trust those new pads that promised to stay put in your panties. Kellie was forced by MGB to wear the old-fashioned menstrual hammock, which truly bordered on being back in "the red tent." In case you don't know what I'm referring to, the menstrual hammock was widely known as a "sanitary napkin." It was a long, rectangular piece of absorbent material suspended between the ill-fated girl's legs by an elastic belt strapped around her waist. To say that this system was inefficient and cumbersome would be a gross understatement. The menstrual hammock hung precariously and unpredictably, shifting and folding, allowing for leaks and embarrassment of huge proportion. It was not an effective option for an overweight, rambunctious 13-year-old girl. But that is what Kellie faced with MGB as her only menstrual mentor.

And what's a girl to do when even the menstrual hammock is not provided? Because it wasn't always available to us. Make your own, of course! Kellie was a real DIY-er and taught me much. One of the most useful skills being how to construct your own feminine hygiene product. This knowledge was invaluable because we were too afraid to ask for real supplies and were never approached to see if we needed any. A whole lot of tape and a wad of paper towels, and voila, you had an instant maxi you could pinch carefully between your legs.

There were other female issues that arose. For example, what about the one and only bra for the two of us to share? Being fair-minded, I believe Kellie and I worked out an amicable arrangement about sharing custody of The Bra. It was 50/50. Every other day, I awoke to see the gray, disintegrating brazier laying across the rocking chair my mother used to rock us to sleep in. Now, instead of holding the comfort of my mother's arms, it held out for me the comfort of a supported bosom for a day.

How about adding on another "new-fangled" thing to deal with, like ADHD? Kellie may have been the first case of this heretofore undocumented disease. The fact that my father worked for a pharmaceutical company meant he could, on occasion, give Kellie samples of the newly marketed drug, Ritalin. She carried the "magic" pills in her purse like mints and had been given the meticulous instruction to take the now-controlled substance "whenever she felt like she needed it." Kellie was at the mercy of her innovation-wary grandmother and her overprescribing father, the ADHD compelling her to wildly fling herself about while taking special care not to rock, quite literally, the "period hammock."

Every day in this fateful summer, Kellie fled our house the first chance she got, but of course, never before our assignments were finished. Rebelliously, she crossed the line one day by leaving a butter knife in the sink. MGB was making her rounds and noticed the infraction as Kellie was already on her way out the back door, about to be whisked away by her friend's mother waiting in the car outside. MGB violently caught hold of Kellie's terrycloth shorts and, without caring who was watching, gave her an atomic wedgie that Kellie would never forget. The pain, not to mention the humiliation, was monumental. Amusing, yet, disturbing.

With my sisters gone, the unbearable lengthiness and emptiness of each day spread out before me. Hunkered in the basement to escape the vast loneliness and extreme heat of the historic home with no air conditioning, the black and white television that once sat mostly unused became my frequent companion. I wasn't too picky about what I watched, but my preference was for old movies or reruns of old shows like Bewitched or Father Knows Best. I loved these shows because I used to watch them when I was home sick from school and my mom was taking care of me. These shows reminded me of happy, normal times. Distracted by television, I didn't have to think about Mommy being sick or dwell on how surreal it was that she was ever really here. I didn't have to worry about my dad coming home and being Scary Guy. And I could put off the near panic attack about who I was going to hang out with once school started, because I was going to have to hang out with somebody. There in the cool darkness, I could divert my thoughts and fears, absorbing obscure movie lines to recite and impress my sisters with randomly.

Obviously, sitting in the basement wasn't the ideal way to spend each day. I knew I had to find a friend, not just to survive the upcoming school year, but to survive the summer! I managed to wrangle a few invitations to hang out with a girl I had known in elementary school. Freedom! But it was sometimes a little too much freedom. Her parents both worked, so we had no supervision.

Her older sister was left in charge and she often had friends over, as well. Being older, they knew things we didn't know, and it wasn't like they tried to protect our innocence.

Once, one of the older boys blew up a condom and tied it to the handlebars of his bike, riding up and down the street with it flapping around, as the crowd went wild.

Was this really better than being at home, buried in the basement? I was felt up by one of the boys who grabbed the pocket on the t-shirt I was wearing.

"Pinch your pocket," he'd quipped, like it was no big deal. Except that he hadn't simply pinched my pocket, he had grabbed my breast! Okay, was this how life was going to be for me now? No parents-just free falling out into the abyss of unsupervised teen angst??

If nothing else, at least there was good food at this friend's house. They had a MICROWAVE! In the early days of microwaves, which this was, they were so big that most people didn't have space for them on their kitchen countertops. Heavy-duty carts on casters became the trendy way to house these monstrosities. My friend's microwave was so big, it had to live on its cart in a separate room.

The gourmet dish of choice from the microwave was "grilled cheese". It wasn't really grilled cheese. It was melted cheese on stone-hard, white bread, all the moisture zapped out by the radioactive kitchen appliance. But it was better than all that nubby bologna I would have been sitting in the basement eating at my house!!

Yes, nubby bologna. Since Grandma spent much of her life worried about money, she had grown accustomed to cutting costs wherever she could. One inventive way was to bypass the grocery store deli department and buy her bologna, the mainstay of any good diet, in bulk.

Grandma bought the giant, cylindrical hunk of bologna and brought it home to cut up - I mean "saw up" herself. She would show those charlatans at the grocery store, who wanted to charge a nice little fee to slice up the meat.

The end result of the DIY slicing was that our bologna sandwiches were an inch and a half thick on one end and gradually disappeared into nothing on the other end.

"Yes, I'd like to order a sawed-off bologna sandwich, please. Oh, and could you make it all fuzzy and nubby by cutting it with a dull serrated knife?"

Bologna Betty earned her most famous name of all in that money-saving, bologna-sawing scheme of hers. Well-played, Bologna Betty. Well-played.

Okay, so why do I go on and on about bologna?

Well, first, it's funny. But second, and most important, the bologna symbolized my life. Yes, I actually said that. It started out just fine, like all other 10-pound cylinders of processed lunch meat. But then it got mutated and hacked apart and never yielded a full portion after that.

And that was what I felt happened to my life once my mom got sick and spent a summer being poisoned in the hospital. Life was forever mutated, hacked off and fuzzy. It would be many, many years before I felt as though I could get a full portion of life or its joy again.

But, let's not get too serious just yet. Because there's plenty more food and fun where Betty was concerned. Like, for instance, the time nine, of the ten, pounds of H.G. Wells bologna "disappeared".

Now Betty and Bart were both equally cynical when it came to us children and what we might be "up to" think "Professor Snape" from *Harry Potter* here. When Betty couldn't find the missing nitrate-infused meat, she promptly KNEW that Kellie and I were the culprits. We must have eaten all that bologna (how many times have I typed the word bologna?).

And so, with Grandma weary from hunting all day for the missing loot, she announced that we were "going to get it" when my father came home! And we did.

Now, let me give you a little background on our beautiful house, so you can fully appreciate the silliness of the sentencing Kellie and I received for the Missing Bologna.

Our house had been meticulously designed and built around the turn of the twentieth century, when there had been a discovery of natural gas in the area. This discovery drew much wealth and notoriety to town, along with many folks who wanted to make a name for themselves. The neighborhood is now listed on the register of historic places to protect and restore these fabulously built homes from an era when taxes were minimal, money was plentiful, and life was good.

Our beautiful home had been the crown jewel of this community. The brick house had two main living floors, and a third floor completely fitted to support a full-time servant staff. The staff living quarters had a separate entrance and the house had multiple stairwells to accommodate their stealth movement. On the two main floors, there were five large bedrooms, one full and one half bath. The grand staircase was interrupted by a spacious, open landing and lined with a full wall of leaded windows to showcase the expansive back yard with its fruit trees, flower gardens, and limestone barbecue and picnic area. The mini mansion also boasted a large butlers' pantry, a morning room, a formal dining room with more of the leaded glass and even had a working servants' buzzer.

People thought we were rich. Maybe we were; I don't know. I'm sure people drove by our impressive home and thought how lucky the family was that lived there. Ah! If they only knew. Not privileged or leading a life of luxury to be sure. We were more like passengers on a train that was being derailed in slow motion.

Inside, we were a family in the process of sustaining a terminal wounding, not yet seeing the full veil of sickness, alcoholism, and fear that we were to be shrouded with. No need to stare folks, keep driving.

So, when my dad came home the day of the Great Bologna Heist, oh boy, Kellie and I were treated to a good, old fashioned punishment.

"If you're gonna eat like pigs, you're gonna live like pigs!" my dad decreed.

And with that, I was kicked permanently out of the room my mother had lovingly and meticulously decorated just for me.

Painstakingly, she had hung the Holly Hobby wallpaper in my room and hand-constructed the delicate, Wedgewood-blue drapes. She, personally, hunted down the perfect antique dresser and bed frame, stripping and staining them a beautiful chocolate brown, making them the show pieces for my little girl bedroom. Mean Grandma Betty had even needle-pointed the two Holly Hobby pictures that were hanging on the wall, back when she could be just a grandmother.

I was told to pack my things into boxes and move into Kellie's room, which, also, had been meticulously decorated, just for her. In fact, every room of this house had been poured over by my mother who was always papering, painting, sanding, staining. You see, everything started out beautiful. Our lives. Our home.

Everything started out perfect, round and full.

And then, out of the blue, the beauty of that house got hacked apart, sawed up into something unrecognizable, for no good reason. Just like that bologna. (I said it again.)

The "pigs" had to live out of cardboard boxes, crammed into one room, even though there was plenty of room and established beauty to go around.

Looking at this now, I see it as the Kicked Out of the Garden Moment that it was. I mean, think Biblically, in Genesis. Everything started out beautiful. God created unparalleled magnificence in the Garden of Eden for His beloved creation, Adam and Eve, to live in. It was perfect. There was unequaled artistry and provision at every turn in the Garden. God, Himself, had prepared it just for them. And then, the serpent came. Adam and Eve believed the lie that God was not providing for them, but was, in fact, holding out on them, trying to keep them from "having it all". Once the lie was bitten into, Adam and Eve were shut out of the Garden, shut out from all the beauty that had been established and provided solely for them.

Of course, as a 12-year-old, I wasn't thinking about Adam and Eve and the Garden of Eden. But as I write this, the analogy is indisputable. Like the snake in the Garden, sickness wound its way into our home and swallowed all the goodness in our lives!

A few months later, Betty found the allegedly scarfed bologna hiding in the freezer, wrapped in aluminum foil, just where she, herself, had put it. Remember me saying poor Betty was in the early stages of dementia? You might be thinking, "Oh, you probably got to move back into your room. Your dad and your grandma apologized to you." But you would be wrong.

You see, the rules were all laid out for my parents in the "Parenting Creed" they subscribed to in the 1970s. There was an explicit subsection that clearly stated: "No authority figure shall weaken his or her position by apologizing for, or admitting, any wrong-doing. Neither shall any figure of authority ask clarifying questions, or entertain the idea that things are not, perhaps, as they seem. Most assuredly, said authority will not give rebel children the benefit of the doubt."

So, Kellie and I stayed right where we were in our little pig sty, pulling clothes out of cardboard boxes, trading off the one gray, broken-down, dingy bra every other day, for some years to come.

But poor Betty. Her senility would materialize a few more times around food. Once, we got in trouble over another meat issue. (Maybe this is where my meat aversion stems from?) Grandma wandered into the living room where we were sitting. Now, the living room was strictly Off Limits, so it must have been Christmas, which was the only sanctioned time to be there.

"Who took the pork chops out of the oven?" she asked, looking absolutely bewildered, a far-off look in her eyes.

Betty had all kinds of concern for pinching pennies and for keeping tabs on where various meats were being stored or cooked, but not much care went into providing for the nurturing we three girls so desperately needed and ached for.

She was a tough cookie, rigidly adhering to her own schedule. The drill sergeant prepared one meal for us kids, a poor man's Shepherd's Pie: instant mashed potatoes made watery and gluey by the canned corn and boiled hamburger that rested on top of the delicious casserole. She did laundry once a week, only on Mondays, and we were forbidden to put our hands on that washing machine, so forget about doing laundry on your own! Forget also about having your gym uniform washed or your one pair of jeans with the blood stain. Nobody gets in to use the washing machine. Not nobody-no how.

Yes, these may seem like little things. Clean clothes. A bra. Maxi pads. But really, are they little? Aren't they instead, really, basic needs?

Chapter 4
My '70s Parents

Mean Grandma Betty was only part of the picture. My father, Bart, was another, more frightening piece, of the family dynamic.

First, however, let me start by sharing insight I've been blessed to receive: My father did the best he could. No one wants to hurt the people they're supposed to be loving. No one starts out and says, "When I grow up, I'm going to be an abusive, alcoholic father." No one does that. In His great mercy, God has shown me that my dad was a hurting soul, with his own painful beginnings to overcome.

Born in West Virginia in 1933, his heartache began during childhood, just like mine. With his father working at Western Union, they were a wealthy family. Daddy was the youngest of five children and was only 7 years old when his own father died. With no life insurance, the Murphys plummeted, instantly, into poverty. Sometime after that, they ended up in the same town where my mom's family had moved.

I'm sure life had been hard for my dad, as a child, but I don't know any specifics because he rarely shared personal stories with us. I know his mother struggled with alcohol. In fact, just before my mom and dad were married, after drinking too much one night, she attempted to retrieve something from the basement. She tripped on the stairs and fell to her death.

My reason for mentioning this is to make the point that Daddy had his own sad story to contend with. The familiar cliché of hurting people hurt people explains a lot.

You see, it shows me where my father's doom and gloom perspective came from. His was a riches to rags story, just like MGB's was. A reversal of what God promised us in His Word. Instead of having beauty for ashes[1], both my parents had seen their beauty turned to ashes through death, divorce, and poverty. As a child, this is exactly what I concluded I would have, as well. Our family stories taught us to be still and wait for the ferocious God above to clamp down and tear our lives into unrecognizable shreds. That is the window through which we all regarded life. And we were mentored in this by Daddy, who certainly had reason to think this was true. This viewpoint was, unfortunately, never fully transformed for my father.

Despite the ugliness of his youth, he experienced temporary beauty in his life when he married my mother. After their wedding, my mom made it her goal to get my dad a Good Job. She typed and sent resume after resume on his behalf, landing him a job with a pharmaceutical company. Daddy started his new job and the happy couple began their new life together.

Bart and Francie were young and fun and ready for the good life that his job and their marriage promised. They liked their martinis and they liked their cigarettes. Think of the popular show Mad Men. That show really hit the mark when it came to depicting life in the 60's.

Many people smoked and drank wherever and whenever they pleased. It was more than socially acceptable. In some circles, especially in the business world, it was socially demanded. In fact, daddy frequently opined that he didn't trust anyone who didn't smoke or drink. As with most newlyweds, their first years together were probably filled with fun and frivolity, but also with some growing pains as they learned to navigate life together. I'm only guessing, but I feel even then, their habit of drinking had to have brought some trouble for them.

My mom had my sister, Marie, two years after they were married. Marie was a beautiful child and seemed, from the few pictures we have, to have been adored by both of them.

How could Marie have grown up anything less than a perfect specimen? After all, Bart and Francie were intelligent people with the financial resources to give Marie all of life's advantages.

Well, let's just point out that having good intentions doesn't a good parenting experience make. (I'm sad to say my daughters will say the same about some of my own parenting choices.) At any rate, we each took with us specific souvenirs of our '70s parents, being affected directly by their outlook.

For example, my father was convinced, as were others in previous generations, that showing a child, even an infant, physical affection, would cause the child to be spoiled and needy. At my father's command, Mommy was forbidden to pick Marie up or show her any physical affection. Over the years, my aunt shared how my mom would sneak into Marie's nursery from time to time to hold her, as my mother was not happy with the arrangement.

A few years later, along came Kellie Sue. Can you see that my dad was *really* into that whole Irish name thing? Mommy was not going to be told she couldn't touch this child. So, she picked up and held and loved Kellie. Kellie would appear to have been perfectly positioned, were it not for the alleged public hatred my sister, Marie, was accused of having for her.

According to family lore, my sister, Marie, was so jealous of Kellie dethroning her as the only child that she tried to kill Kellie. Mmmm hmmmm. This story was part of the oral history passed on regularly.

So, recall that Daddy was a pharmaceutical representative or "drug rep" right? This is back before there were any rules or regulations about prescription medication samples. This is back, therefore, when a drug rep was, in his own rights, the local shaman. And maybe that's what Bart Murphy really was. Maybe that's why he drank so much. To get a vision from the gods.

All I can tell you is that, for our family, he was the doctor. I could have counted the number of times I went to see a real doctor as a kid. True, I saw plenty of them come stumbling upstairs during my mom and dad's parties. But to actually employ the expertise of a doctor when I was sick? No need. That butler's pantry I mentioned earlier wasn't just storing silver and serving trays for dinner parties. It was also stuffed with prescription samples.

Because the drug reps had the opportunity to hang out at each other's car trunks and trade samples of medicines, new and old. Although it sounds shocking to us now, when we have to sign an affidavit to get some cold medicine, in the '70s, this bartering was perfectly legal.

"Hey, do you have any Elavil samples? I'm having trouble sleeping." Or, "Do you have any Ritalin samples, my kid's driving me crazy!" The drug reps game of "Go Fish". It was that sort of thing.

As the story goes, Marie found some pills in the basement and dutifully fed them to Kellie, only a baby, who would've eaten just about anything. It wouldn't have been odd that my dad had samples of "water pills," as my mom used to call them, which were diuretics. Dangerous? Absolutely. Do I think Marie was trying to kill Kellie? No. I think Marie was about 4 years old and saw these nice "candies" and gave them to the baby. This part of the story is believable.

But in the Irish world, where a good story is truly a treasure, you always exaggerate, making the story a little juicier each time you tell it. Wait a minute...is that an exaggeration?

The reason the story falls apart for me is the motive my parents assigned Marie for giving Kellie the "candy."

"Marie, you hate Kellie. You've always hated Kellie. You tried to poison her when she was just a baby."

Really? We think a toddler tried to kill a baby? This is amusing? This is another of those bad choices on the part of those '70s parents of ours that had long- lasting consequences. But to my mom and dad, having a good story to tell seemed to be more important than protecting the children the story was about.

Here's another fun '70s parent story.

"Marie, you hated Kellie so much that when your mom was pregnant with her, you used to jump up and down on her stomach because you wanted to kill the baby."

Ha-ha! It's just good clean fun, right?

I think that rather than being amusing, being told over and over that you hate your sister so much you tried to kill her could have a bad effect on your relationship with the sister you "tried to kill," at the least, and at the most, could affect how you see yourself for having "tried to kill" that sister. I'm just saying. Marie and Kellie have always had to work extra hard to get along. Could this be because of the stories of the young, murderous Marie? I don't know. But I know for sure these stories didn't promote family unity!

Where do I fit into all of this? Well, I know a little more about this than I care to.

I was probably about 8 years old when I came across a postcard of a seedy-looking motel. "What is this place?" I asked my mom.

"Oh, that's the motel where you were conceived," she answered in a rare moment of personal candor.

A mere two months after Perfectly-positioned Kellie had been born, my parents stole away on a "date night" and, well, here I am.

So, that's another reason why you can get rid of that whole "Perfectly-positioned" Kellie notion.

Kellie quickly became "The Thing that My Mother Tried to Put Down".

"Here, sit over here and eat a cookie. I'm pregnant and I can't even think about taking care of you right now."

"Sit here and eat this. I'm overwhelmed and nauseous."

And who wouldn't be overwhelmed to find out you're

pregnant when you still have a two-month-old in the bassinet? I get it! I don't blame my mom for trying to find a place to put Kellie while she desperately tried to figure out what to do about the impending doom of another child.

But hey, let's not forget my mom was pregnant in the 60's and it was completely acceptable, even medically encouraged, for her to have all the martinis and ciggies she wanted. And she did. I was born dangerously underweight, perhaps due to this medical advice. But this was easily fixed for me with a few extra days in the hospital, while Kellie became a lifelong victim of my mom's habit of preoccupying her with food.

Now my parents weren't oblivious to Kellie's weight issue. They never hid their revulsion, always putting her on diets and incentivizing her weight loss.

"If you lose 10 pounds, we'll get you the new Carpenters' album," they promised.

Ten pounds lost. Check. Carpenter album in hand, twelve pounds gained back. Check. Kellie repetitively lost 10 pounds to get whatever thing had been promised her, and then, religiously, gained back the 10 pounds plus a few more.

Why 10 pounds? Why was this the golden number? I know it couldn't have been doctor's orders because remember, we didn't go to the doctor. I'm going to assert that my mom held, firmly, the reins on the food supply, and there should never have been a reason to have to play, "Let's Make a Deal" with Kellie about her weight. I hate to say it, but putting the onus of Kellie's weight control on her 10-year-old self may have stemmed from selfishness on my mom's part. You see, Bart and Francie had the happy hour thing going every night and that would've had to have been cut short in order to prepare dinner.

She either wasn't willing to make that sacrifice, or, she was fearful of daddy's reaction if she left his company to take care of us. Either way, while they were "bonding" in the den over cocktails, we kids would be risking life and limb outside the sacred entryway of my father's den, trying stealthily to get my mom's attention, to let her know we were HUNGRY! An informal vote would be taken on who was going to convey the message of potential starvation. It was widely held that I was my mom's favorite. Due to this allegation, I was usually the one elected to roll onto the scene, just outside the door of the exclusive, invitation-only room, rubbing my stomach and making my eyes big and doe-like, trying hard to take on the qualities of what I imagined a starving child would have.

Finally seeing me, Mommy would give the nearly imperceptible nod, so as not to alert my father that we were anywhere in the vicinity. This slight movement meant, "Yes, it's okay if you break into the Snack Drawer."

Now, do you see the lengths we went to in order to get the "all clear" for food?

So, it stands to reason that my mom had solid control over our food intake. It clearly wasn't like we were gathering around that beloved "Snack Drawer" and eating willy-nilly.

No, you had to have Special Clearance to get into the Snack Drawer. It was by invitation only.

So, I'm just saying, if this was the case, why was my sister so overweight?

Why didn't my mom just tell her, "No, you can't have any junk food. I will make you a healthy dinner and feed you at a healthy time." How about that for a strategy? Hmmmm......nah!

The best deal they ever made Kellie, the deal that truly epitomized our quirky '70s parents?

"Kellie, if you lose 10 pounds, we'll buy you a 10-pound box of chocolate."

Chapter 5
The Reunion

It was a wintery day when I sat in the auditorium, still, at this point, at the rundown school. My mom's cancer was back, but I didn't know yet that she'd be removed from our home and our lives for the entirety of the upcoming summer. However, I did know that things seemed to be getting very serious with her health again.

Since it was too cold to go outside like we normally did after lunch, the powers in charge thought it would be good clean fun for the kids to pass the time in the auditorium, playing records, which we were encouraged to bring in. Most of the girls were on stage, carefree and uninhibited, spontaneously choreographing a dance to "Hot Child in the City."

I vividly recall this particular afternoon and that I was not carefree or unencumbered like the girls dancing on the stage. All by myself in one of the rows of empty seats, with my short, thick, frizzy hair helmet, wearing a scratchy, wool sweater, I was cold with the thought, "What if Mommy dies?!"

But I couldn't imagine this actually happening.

I did my best to conjure up, in my mind, what life would look like if my mom died. But, I couldn't picture it. I couldn't even get a shadowy image of what would happen to me. And so, I reasoned: "Well, if I can't picture it, it's not going to happen."

That certainty, derived from my own lack of understanding and cognitive development, would be the cause of a lot of trouble for me later. It was because of that naïve conclusion that I came to feel betrayed by God, and myself. The experience taught me to work harder at imagining all the terrible things I thought could or might happen. If I could see these mental pictures all the way through, and endure the anxiety that would rear up behind them, then I would be safe. It was what I could not imagine or rehearse that had proven to be a danger to me.

Later, when the summer of MGB and Chemotherapy was coming to a close, my mom, it was widely rumored, would finally be coming home! I couldn't wait.

Finally, our life would get back to normal!

We would have our mom back, and we desperately needed her! Big things were happening for us. Kellie clearly needed to be rescued from Grandma's Period Hammock. She had already tried to remedy this predicament herself by buying and "installing" a super plus tampon. The thinking was: go with the biggest one they make so you don't have to keep putting a new one in. This turned into a disaster of nearly the Hindenburg size! Kellie sat in the bathroom and cried as she tried to remove the super-sized tampon from her virgin body that would not let go of it.

And don't forget: (I won't let you!) I was going to a new school in just a few short weeks and I needed help!!! I had no clothes that fit or shoes without holes in them. I looked like I had stuck my finger in a light socket and my hair had responded to the trauma as expected, by being stiff and coarse and sticking straight out from my head like Bozo the Clown. The absurdity of my appearance was frequently pointed out to me by Daddy, yet no solutions had ever been offered up. I needed a momma!!

"The Parents of Bridget Murphy" had gotten an official letter from the Nice School. How was the school administration to know that I, at least temporarily, was caught without parents? The correspondence sat dangerously unopened on the heap of all the rest of the mail that remained unopened because Daddy was so busy making sure his wife didn't die while he commuted from work to the hospital and back home, day after day.

I was uneasy as I waited for the urgent contents to be revealed, but could in no way advance the cause, for fear of attracting the unwanted attention and anger of Daddy. When the letter was finally unsealed, I spied that it detailed the exact t-shirt and shorts I would need for gym class at the Nice School and where to buy them. This errand, I understand now, was not at the top of my dad's "to do" list. But it sure was on the tip top of mine!

I was terrified to show up in anything less than standard fare, because I already had enough working against me. And trust me, you do not want me to even begin to draw for you the trauma that was middle school gym class in 1970-something. I'll give you a vague picture. There was a massive "shower room" where all gym participants were forced to strip naked and join in the shower party full of perfect girls and a scrutinizing gym teacher. That's where I will leave that discussion, other than to add that, today, this would be considered child abuse, if not child pornography. Oh my, it was dreadful!

So, yeah, I thought Mommy was coming home and it

would be time to hop in the car and go shopping and tackle these life details that had piled up after three months. We'd been living like urchins for the whole summer and it was showing! Do you remember those little kids in the movie "Chitty, Chitty, Bang, Bang" who were kidnapped by the creepy Candy Man? Remember how dirty and forlorn they were after living under the castle, away from their parents? Well, that was us! It was high time we had our momma back so life could go back to normal.

No one prepared us for what we were about to experience when my mom came home at the end of that summer. However, there was a lot going on to prepare the *house* for her arrival.

Friends of my mom stopped by all morning and cloistered themselves off with my grandma, discussing the day's big event. They didn't have bouquets of flowers with them or banners with sentiments like: "Welcome Home!" or "You did it!" I presumed the celebration was low key because nobody else was as excited as I was to have Mommy back.

I remembered another time she had come home from the hospital a few years earlier. She had met Kellie and I at the front door, presented us with a "Snack n' Cake", and the three of us assembled on the brown plaid couch to watch the "ABC After School Special" together. Granted, that little extravaganza had followed a much shorter hospital stay, not like this 3-month absence she was returning from, but it was my only reference point. I could only assume this was going to be a similar reunion.

Seeing one of mom's girlfriends struggle to get up the front porch steps with a portable toilet, I began to wonder just what was going on here. Why were they putting a toilet in my mom's exquisitely appointed bedroom? A foam, egg-crate mattress cover replaced the heavy, velvet bedspread my mom had made. This, I was told by my cousin, was to keep her from getting bed sores. The food and drink for this party was nowhere near the Great Gatsby Party menu from just a year ago. Cans of jellied protein lined the shelves and displaced some of the drugs in the butler's pantry. Fresca was the cocktail of choice for the guest of honor, not the usual martini.

Never, at any time, did anyone gather up my sisters and me, and say, "Look, your mom is really weak and really sick. Don't expect the person you remember to pull up here today." The only information I had about her stay in the hospital was that Marie had been excused from weekly, mandatory church attendance, because after seeing my mom, she didn't believe in God anymore.

Okay, call me stupid, but I wasn't putting it all together. Why would I? I was 12 and had no idea what "chemo" was or that you could actually poison a person, just to the edge of death, on purpose, and then send her home to be the mom.

Nor did anyone gather us up and say, "We love you. This is going to be hard for you. But we're going to be okay. We'll get through this."

To my dad and grandma, and all the other adults, this *was* none of our business. We didn't need to know about the porta-potty because that was my mom's business and who did we think we were?

"Who do you think you are?" was a question that was frequently falling angrily out of Daddy's mouth, usually accompanied with the thudding of his stubby, meaty finger into my chest.

"Nobody, sir,"

"That's right," he would confirm.

To their minds, we had no horse in this race. We didn't need to know. We were nobody. We didn't matter. It was none of our business. Our job was to make sure the AstroTurf was freshly groomed and stay out of the way.

In front of our stately home, the former neighborhood destination, the car pulled up to deposit the woman who was once not only the life of the party, but the life of this home.

Like ants swarm around a crumb of food to obscure it and transport it, Mommy's and Daddy's friends huddled around the car to extract the limp body inside. Formed into a group, they had Mommy seated across their arms in a fireman's carry. Two people awkwardly squatted with their arms stretched to meet the others, while Mommy sat on the seat that was created from their extended arms being locked together.

With her own arms lifelessly hanging over the carriers' shoulders, there was a friend, no doubt feeling very important, spotting Mommy from behind, hands pressed lightly against her back to keep the frail woman from toppling backward. The visitors who were non-essential to carrying the inanimate patient walked alongside this huddled mass, in what I thought, even at the time, looked like the scene from the final episode of "Mary Tyler Moore"[4], where the cluster of friends moved in unison to fetch the Kleenex box. Our faithful Cockapoo, Shanty, was also excited to see the person who had been MIA, but, unfortunately, he got a little too close to the transport team. He was sent flying by someone's forceful foot. When the team finally transferred my mom into her favorite chair on the porch, they backed away slowly and cautiously, the way you do when you hang a picture and you're not sure it will stay where you put it. The remnant of a person who used to be my mom was finally revealed.

There are no words to describe the person deposited in that chair. She had on a stiff, synthetic, butterscotch-colored wig that looked like it had been doused with baby powder. It was too big for her and dwarfed her face even more than the months of poison coursing through her veins already had. Like a poster child for starving children in a third world country, her teeth protruded from her hollowed-out face, ghoulishly, making her look like an eerie, preposterous caricature of herself. Her skin and her eyes were dull, matted, and she did not speak or even look at us.

What would have been helpful to know was that she was probably on heavy duty painkillers, like morphine. I am just now, as I write this, realizing this was probably the case. Of course, she would have been drugged to endure the long ride home and the anxiety of the homecoming.

But we should have been told that! I guess it was none of our business. We were left to think that Mommy wasn't happy to see us or happy to be home. I thought she didn't care, that she hadn't missed us all those months. She didn't reach out to us, or attempt to reassure us that she was okay, or that she missed us or loved us. She just stared off, vacantly.

"Are you all right, Francie?" "What can I get you, Francie?" the rubberneckers chirped.

"Do you want something to drink, Francie?"

Because a drink was the common cure in these parts for anything that ailed you, though Mommy's beverage would no longer contain alcohol. Nevertheless, old habits dictated that we get that woman a drink!

"Go get your mother some Fresca!" someone commanded.

That was the touching reunion. The beloved dog was cruelly punted across the porch. We were shooed out of the way and told to stop staring at the nearly dead woman who now seemed like an unwilling participant in this homecoming.

"Get your mother a Fresca!" Grandma hissed at me.

In I went to get the vessel of the trendy soft drink, which was quite pointless, because Mommy was too weak to lift the glass to her mouth.

There was not going to be any "After School Special" watching, no snuggling up, no tutorials on how to use a tampon, and no buying a gym uniform.

"This is bad," my brain told me.

No tender beautiful moments of seeing our mother again. Just fear and dread and devastatingly harsh reality. That was early August.

My mom always thought there had to be some hidden meaning that all of our major family moments, marriages and births, had been in August. Just two weeks later, at the end of that month, laying in her bed, waiting for the ambulance that had been urgently called to take her back to the hospital, she thought she had it figured out. To my cousin, who had come to help take care of her, she pleaded, as the stretcher maneuvered past me, where I stood on the stairs, "Please don't take me to the hospital. I'll die!" she begged weakly with big, fat tears running down her cheeks.

But that didn't happen. Not yet.

The Fat, Frizzy-haired girl earned her official title precisely as the academic year at the Nice School barreled in.

Each morning, I woke up early to manage the woolly mess on my head. Chubby, still with a slightly detectable lisp and crooked teeth, I looked exactly like I felt. Disheveled. Abandoned. Hopeless. Alone. Pointless.

From a beautiful and promising beginning, and despite the apparent wealth of my father, there I was in this place where every other child seemed to be loved and taken care of, as I lisped along, in my one pair of menstrual-stained jeans and bristled mane, heralding that I was not loved, not cared about.

The girls at my new school had silky, feathered hair pulled into side ponytails, just like Chrissy Snow on Three's Company[5]. They had "outfits". They had lunches packed. They had hair ribbons! For crying out loud! Someone cared enough about these girls, loved them so much, they even had ribbons in their hair! And there I was.

I knew how bad I looked, even then. But it was decades later that this was confirmed. When I was well-settled into adulthood, my stepmother, Karen, came to visit and, for some reason, she requested to see my high school yearbook. I obliged and dug out the dusty treasure, when something fluttered out, onto the deck, where we were sitting.

Only knowing something had fallen out but not exactly what, I picked it up and was stricken, my mouth had that surge of saliva you get just before you throw up. I hadn't seen this picture in twenty two years. And I had spent those decades putting as much emotional distance between me and the Fat, Frizzy-haired girl in the picture as possible.

"Oh!" I said sadly, "This is my school picture from 7th grade."

Taking it from my hand, Karen laughed and guffawed and berated the pathetic girl in the picture.

"Oh, you oughta hang that picture in your basement. It'll scare the mice away!"

She was so mean about it that I wanted to hit back.

"That was the year my mom died," I lobbed flatly, certain that would put her in her place - that she would feel bad for ridiculing me for something which should've drawn consolation and compassion from her.

"I hardly see what that has to do with your picture," she said, coolly, looking directly eye to eye with me, her tone suddenly serious.

"Are you kidding me?" I wanted to shout. "It has everything to do with it!"

Over the years, I had remained completely dumbfounded by the fact that none of the adults in our world acknowledged that we children had our own story in this tragedy of my mom's. That there were lots of "sub-tragedies" happening underneath the main one of my mother, like a skyscraper falling in on itself, after the initial blast from the demolition crew.

Standing on the deck with Karen that day as she got her jollies from my suffering, I wanted that tragedy acknowledged. I wanted someone to say, "You poor thing! That must have been so hard!"

The image of that pathetically disheveled and sorrowful girl in the school picture stirred up the anger I had at the people who could have taken care of us. Why didn't they regard caring for Francie's daughters as an extension of caring for Francie?

It isn't vanity that ignited my emotional reaction to the school picture. It was that my appearance in that picture was *symptomatic* of the loss Francie's daughters were bearing.

No one considered *our* loss. Not just the loss of our mother, but of our place in the Garden and the beauty it afforded. Our loss of stability and of all the little things that come with having a momma around, like making sure you *look* like somebody loves you!

I heard somewhere that children are the "forgotten mourners" and that resonates with me.

Professing, and perhaps even believing: "You're young; you'll get over it," the adults that controlled our world minimized and negated our own intense grief and sorrow because we were young. They, quite simply, looked past us.

Entering the Nice School that first day, it wasn't looking different from the other girls that brought the tight lump in my throat. It was what that difference in appearance prompted me to understand in that moment. The sudden knowledge and sure comprehension that everyone here was loved, but I was not. The certainty of this epiphany was tactile, touchable, as it washed over me, and I can still call it up, even today.

The sickness and imminent death of the one who loved us, along with the rejection from the one we would be left with, would disqualify me forever from the life the silky-haired girls would get to have.

Of course, I didn't specifically understand the symbolism my hair took on. I just knew I had to at least try to look like the other girls. Each night, I methodically coated my stiff tresses with an egg/mayonnaise mixture, the only hair product available to me, and carefully wrapped my head with plastic wrap to let the concoction do its magic. After the potion had time to do its work, I contorted myself over the tub to rinse the thick mess down the drain. Then, out came the orange hairdryer with the comb attachment and I literally pulled my hair dry, stretching it into straight submission.

The next step in my grooming ritual was to don the blue, scratchy ski cap that MGB had, at some point in our former lives, made for me, and then it was off to bed to get my "beauty" sleep. I would rest my hatted head and sleep an unsettled sleep, waiting for Daddy, who sometimes crashed through my bedroom door.

You see, while I was upstairs getting "beautiful", Daddy would be spending time downstairs soothing the horrific ache of a man who was watching his wife die way too young. The martinis that were the chosen prescription for the Medicine Man were abandoned at some point and he switched to whiskey, citing that gin tended to make him mean. Let me assure you, whiskey did not make him any gentler.

All of that numbing before bed sometimes made him

stagger, confused, into the Bologna Twins' room. I would pretend to be asleep, barely even breathing, waiting for him to realize he was in the wrong room and stumble off to his own bed, to lay next to his drugged and dying wife.

I wondered what he might be thinking about down there, soaked in whiskey. Was he sad or angry? Was he remembering the good times? The bad times? I wondered if he ever felt guilt for the way he treated my mom, us. Maybe it was his guilt that made him mean.

Eventually, morning rolled around and I would wake up and remove the gilded cap. The skies would part and the angels would sing and my hair would be straight and flat and absolutely STUCK to my head.

All the better! Now this coiffure would win me friends and influence people. Dressed in my grisly jeans, off I would go, out the door, into the darkness of morning. I walked the mile or so to school and joined the other girls who dutifully gathered in the bathroom to tend to their satin-ribboned coiffures.

There they stood, gossiping about this boy or that dance, with the short, stubby-handled combs nestled into their back pockets, much the way girls now keep their phones with them. I would move in front of the mirror, ready to see my smooth, flattened locks.

Inevitably, in the humidity of the morning, the flat, straight hair had gone "POOF!" on the way to school. An explosion of stiff, thick, unmoving wool roosted on my long thin face, mocking me in the girls' bathroom right in front of the silky girls. So much for that magic hair. Curse that Fat, Frizzy-haired girl!! Always ruining the picture I had in my mind of how I wished things could be.

Despite its shortcomings, it was this routine I had embraced for the first few months of school that year. Another routine my mom wanted us to make part of our mornings was kissing her goodbye. But outside their bedroom, my father would practically threaten our lives if we dared to disturb her. So, we went with the dictator's wishes and did not say good bye to my mom.

Years later, I found out my mom wanted us to say goodbye to her before we left each morning because she wasn't sure she would be alive when we got home. Before she realized my dad was throwing a block outside her door, she would lay in her bed each morning, waiting for us. It must've destroyed her that we never came.

Once, so sad that I hadn't come to kiss her goodbye, she somehow got her feeble body to the window to watch me walk down the street. She was so weak; I have no idea how she managed to get herself hoisted out of the bed. But, she was at the window and I saw her that morning, leaning all her weight on the windowsill, looking small and desperate.

You see, just as she looked for me in the morning, I would look for her. It was common for me to stare up at her bedroom window, leaving home in the dark morning, trying to fathom what was happening in that dark, closed-off, private room.

As she tried to get back to bed, she pushed herself from the window sill with too much zeal, and fell over the portable toilet, knocking it over and spilling the stale liquid onto the mauve carpeting. She lay in the urine until MGB finally heard her crying for help. This image, still, is nearly unbearable for me.

Just before Christmas, we were studying Russia in social studies. The big event in this class, which was highly anticipated by every 7th grader, was the Cultural Tasting Party, and it was rapidly approaching. The teacher assigned partners to work on recipes together after school. A classmate and I were assigned to make a Russian cookie, very much like a shortbread.

So it was that I did not go home from school that afternoon, but went, instead, to my social studies partner's house, to make the cookies. I was thrilled, because, as any girl knows, in middle school, having a Best Friend is crucial to surviving. It sets the tone for the next 6 years of school. I would frequently go to church and get on my knees, pleading with God to send me a best friend, which seemed to be another unanswered prayer.

If I had a best friend, I could manage this mess life had handed me. I fantasized about a best friend the way some girls fantasized about a boyfriend. The fun we would have, the real-life musical montages that would define our Best Friend-ism. But since I had that unfortunate detour, caused by the mystical school boundary lines, when I finally got to the Nice School, all the Best Friend Pairs were already made. I was one year late to that party. I was forced to be on the prowl for someone who was, perhaps, unsatisfied with the Best Friend arrangement they were currently in.

Unfortunately for me, few of the girls were seeking new friendships. They didn't have a lot of interest in bringing me into the fold. The closest I had gotten to the Hair Ribbon Wearers, so far, was that we all walked home in the same general direction. One pivotal day, the Chief Ribbon Wearer, walking directly behind me, noticed the partially concealed, old blood stain, turned green with age, on the back of my only pair of jeans.

What can I say? It was a result of mismanaging the entrepreneurial maxi pad on my part, along with the dastardly master plan MGB employed to only do laundry on Mondays, nullifying any possibility of my getting even a layer of that old blood removed. I simply slipped the filthy jeans on each day with the very purposeful goal of not fretting over the stain, since there was absolutely no way for me to remedy it.

"Is that a **BLOOD** stain on your pants?" the Ribbon Wearer bellowed and they all cackled behind me, murmuring, whispering, and snickering about my dire situation. This marked what I believe must have been, the final lock down on my chances of winning over any unsatisfied friends.

But a girl can dream, and so it was with profound hope and optimism that maybe, just maybe, this frizzy-haired girl would finish this school project with a new best friend that I set off on the cookie-making venture after school that day.

My hopes were dashed after we made the dough for the foreign pastries. I recall, clearly, my horror when I looked at the cookie sheet and saw my new best friend candidate had formed the dough into the shape of the male reproductive system.

First, let me confess that although I knew something was up, I didn't actually know what this shape represented. Potential Friend's ridiculous laughter clued me into the fact that I was missing something here. She blurted out a few crude words to enlighten me, shaming my ignorance with her laughter because she must've known I didn't understand.

It is? I thought. It is? Oh yeah, right, it is! Yeah, I'm cool. I know what this is! Sure. I'll make one too. Heh heh. See, I can fit in!

While I obligingly made my own inappropriate cookie, thinking, maybe I don't want to keep this classmate in the running to be my Best Friend after all, the phone rang. It was somebody from my house, although I don't remember who, telling me that my mom had been taken to the hospital.

That's the end of the memory trail. I can remember the unsettling cookie, but I can't remember the last time I kissed my cherished momma good-bye. I went home not knowing I would never be able to recall the last time I saw her alive.

Chapter 6
The Christmas Dress

The next day after school, after the Russian cultural day that no longer held any allure for me, Daddy came home from the hospital to talk to us.

"Your mother isn't going to make it," he said softly. This was the first official word we had heard of a terminal prognosis.

"Do you want to go and see her at the hospital?" he offered. "Before you answer, she won't know you're there. She looks really bad and she's not awake."

Okay, well, given that we got no heads-up when our macabre mother was carried up looking like a Holocaust survivor a few months ago, and you're telling us that she, indeed, looks bad today, I think I'll pass. My thinking was that I didn't want to remember her that way. So, Kellie and I declined the invitation to the hospital.

As a grown woman now, with children of my own, this decision haunts me. Okay, we didn't want to see my mother, so that we could preserve our memory of her. But what about my mom? I am sure she wanted to see us. Maybe she was conscious and maybe she wasn't. But she would have known her children were there. We should've gone. We should've given her that.

Instead, we stayed home while wave after wave of her friends came over and sat at the house with us for brief periods. One friend came with her older daughter and brought us pizza. I remember the daughter saying, "I hate this waiting."

I remember thinking, "Wait. What are we waiting for?" I didn't get it. I mean, Daddy told us Mommy wasn't going to make it, but it just wouldn't go into my brain. I couldn't process this sentence and all the activity in the house that came with those words.

A few hours went by and Daddy appeared briefly at home again. I recall that I was wearing a light pink, baby-doll nightgown with soft blue ties along the neck, a last remnant sweetly purchased, just for me, by my mom in the good old days. Since it was Christmas time, we were watching Frosty the Snowman when the Medicine Man came into the room, still wearing his dreadful brown corduroy and faux fur coat, wet from the snowy night. He had something in his hand.

"Here," he said, "take this. It'll help you sleep."

He handed my sister, Kellie and I, an Elavil, a hardcore drug for depression and anxiety. You may think it strange to give 12 and 13-year-old girls benzodiazepines, but I told you, it was the '70s! And my dad was the resident physician. So, like good girls, we took our Elavil and went to bed.

The next thing I remember is being woken up in the room where the Bologna Sisters slept. Our twin beds were being held as headquarters for the delivery of The Bad News. My dad, my sister, Marie, and my cousin were sitting on our beds, with the light of the giant outdoor, plastic Christmas candles Kellie and I had hooked up in our bedroom, to ensure ourselves it was, indeed, Christmas, illuminating their destroyed faces.

"She's gone'" my dad said flatly.

And that was that.

The Garden gates were officially closed and we were officially exiled from the beautiful, full life of breakfast outings and family vacations and arguing about silly things like taking up too much room in the backseat.

To my mother's funeral, I wore a green, tartan plaid jumper that Mommy, herself, had picked out for me while she lay in her death bed in the closed-up, mysterious room. She had requested the Sears catalog so she could Christmas shop for her daughters, in rare moments of being nausea free and of a clear mind without the ever-present pain. Intended as a Christmas present, she had not known the dress would be presented to me to wear to her funeral.

Opening the package handed to me and lauded as "an early Christmas gift", I couldn't see clearly with the tears flooding my eyes and the taste of salty mucous dripping into my mouth. The heavy, heavy weight sitting in my stomach would be lodged there for decades to come, as I imagined Mommy, propped up in her bed, half-dead, pointing to this and that item in the catalog, with a devoted friend taking notes.

For the last two years, my mom's duties as a caretaker had been long forgotten, and no one had bought us clothes. This is quite understandable. An unanticipated consequence of a momma becoming terminally ill. The kids have no clothes or shoes that fit them, and it looks like no one loves them. But, she made sure we had Christmas gifts to open that year. It would be the last time we had a tree and presents, but we didn't know that then.

The only one who loved me died. I was left behind with a father who openly spoke of his dislike for me and of whom I was terrified.

Brokenness is the word I would use to describe the years that followed. So broken.

A few people tried to help out here and there, but that didn't last long.

Actually, the day of the funeral I recall a friend of my mom's trying to "help" by taking down the antique picture hanging in the kitchen that said, "What is a home without a mother?"

I watched her stealthily expunge the ironic painting, as if she could just extinguish all the coming wretchedness of that home without the mother, by simply carrying the sentiment away, as if we wouldn't notice it had ever been there, just a blank space on the wall, the way you can't quite tell what's different when someone shaves off a mustache. Something's gone. Something's different. But what?

She hid it in the strange, sloping closet that was nestled under the splendid staircase of our regal home. I followed close behind her and once the deed was done, I kneeled in the closet, in front of the picture.

"Everything that was, is gone," the tight mass in my

throat told me. The magnificent love and care my mom conferred on her family and our home was gone. And I was under the distinct impression I would never experience the manifestations of that kind of love again.

Our family, maybe because we were so entrenched in Irish culture, or maybe because we were so concerned about what was socially expected and accepted in the dysfunctional decade that was the 1970s, had such a strange way of moving forward without Francie Murphy, and all of the other future, albeit smaller, catastrophes nestled around that big one.

"Open casket for the family only!" Daddy announced, like it was a treat that only family would be privy to see. Once the family had seen my mom, the casket was to be closed. Our neighbor had gotten wind of this arrangement and came over to protest just before we left for the funeral home, dressed in our Christmas dresses.

This sad neighbor was another picture of another victim of the '70s. She had been a frequent party guest at our home in years past. She came to be known, even by the kids in the neighborhood, as a heavy, heavy drinker. Life at her house was just as broken at it was at ours. It was just concealed less effectively.

My parents, and some of their peers, thought they could live the way they did, with no consequences. The smoking, the drinking. The not acknowledging problems, emotions and anxieties. Just covering right over them with denial and substances and distractions. Don't get me wrong. I get the motivation for it. There were not many viable antidepressants at the time; that didn't come until the early 80's. There may have been counselors, but not many people would be willing to commit the social suicide that would surely come with the decision to pursue it, were it ever to get out. There was no understanding of mental health and how prevalent depression and anxiety was. And there didn't seem to be any deep seeking of God, Himself, in good times or bad. Why would they have sought Him out? They knew what I knew about Him. He was mad at us. So, He was not a source to seek for comfort!

So, some turned to the socially sanctioned and celebrated means of self-medicating to escape, if even for a few hours, the turmoil they felt inside. But there was a price to pay for the soothing and stuffing. "Lifestyle" diseases like lung cancer, esophageal cancer, emphysema, cirrhosis of the liver are a result, and sometimes a cause, of death.

Years after Mommy died, this woman would have her voice box removed, to stall the path of the cancer that was gobbling up her throat. She would stop over on rare occasions and scare the pants off of us with her mechanical larynx.

But on this day, the day we were to drag over to see my mom in her shiny casket, no one knew how her story would turn out. On this day, our sweet, sad neighbor was just working to express her grief and her anger at not being able to see my mom at the funeral home.

Cleary distraught and stamping her feet, having a tantrum there in our living room, she yelled, "It's not fair!! I wanna see her!" the slurred speech betraying her, giving evidence that she was well into her daily dose of liquid medicine.

Daddy thought an open casket was nothing more than voyeurism, a way to gawk at the dead, and he would not be budged by an emotional bystander, or anyone else, to have the casket open to the public later that day.

We, as a family, were to go into the funeral home to look at the last remains of our sweet momma. So strange. I have since learned that seeing the person after they have died is an important step in dealing with grief and the endless cycle of grieving. Seeing that person that you love laid out in their best dress tells the brain, in the surreal days and months that follow, that yes, this did happen. I get it. Because later, for me, it seemed not real that my mom was ever really alive.

"She's in the big room," the funeral director told us when we arrived. My dad, ever the nickname giver, coined him "Mr. Crayola" because of the colorful, mismatched clothes he wore.

"We anticipate a big turn out," Mr. Crayola said, with a sparkle in his eye. What a strange thing to be energized by. But, that was his job.

Wearing my plaid funeral jumper, chosen for me by the deceased, my clearest recollection is wanting to get this dreaded Important Step over. I felt awkward, and didn't know what I should do or say as I ventured alone and ignorant into the Big Room. The picture I have of her, confiscated by death, is not detailed.

She lay in the casket with that awful wig I had first seen when she made the death march back home just a few months earlier. She was hollowed out and vacant. Not real. Not at all like the woman I remembered, who used to look up from whatever she was doing to say brightly, "Hi baby!" whenever I came near.

The only thing that protected me was that none of it

seemed real. I was a moveable action figure that was being handled by something bigger than I was, hypnotically taking one step after the other, toward the long box with the wigged head sticking out the top.

In my rush to leave the room, I was caught by Marie, who eased me onto her lap in the lobby. I towered over her petite little frame and cried.

As a 16-year-old girl at the time Mommy died, Marie would struggle for years to come, wrestling with the relationship she didn't have with my mother. My mom dying at that point in Marie's life ripped a huge hole that only God Himself would be able to fill in and heal. But we didn't know that then. We didn't know the long, long journey we all had yet to take. We just needed to get through this day.

Mr. Crayola's prediction had been accurate. It was standing room only for this viewing. The block was circled by people waiting in line to see my mother. Only the joke was on them, they were not actually going to be able to see her. Seeing the grieving family is a good by-product, I suppose. Please don't get me wrong, I was grateful they had come. But it just seems gruesome. Like rubbernecking as you drive by a fatal car accident. I think when people see such tragedy and realize it has not struck them, they have a false sense of security against any such trauma coming to their own door.

Plus, I think whenever someone dies so prematurely, a crowd always comes around. My mother was only 45 years old, and left behind 3 young daughters. She seemed to have it all. She left behind the life that so many people assumed they knew and wanted. They didn't know the paradox we lived in. People saw glamor and notoriety.

The beauty outside concealed the deep core of alcoholism and abuse underneath - like wearing designer clothes, but having filthy, stained and torn underwear. Just so everything LOOKS good! This was the brokenness behind our door and it would eat up more of our inside in the years ahead.

They say that when a woman gives birth, she can't remember the pain of doing so. That it becomes a distant memory. And thank God, because if women truly remembered the pain, there would probably be a lot less people in this world.

But, isn't this numbing to pain true across all of life? We experience the most gripping, searing pain. And then, we walk on and away. Numb. In shock. Forgetful of what was and, mercifully, ignorant to what lies ahead.

And that is what we did. We went on. After the wake, where about one hundred people filled our home to the edges, gathered around the keg - I'm not kidding - commiserating, they all went home. And that was that. We were left in the pit of What Had Been.

Have you ever seen the hole that is left after a big, healthy tree is dug up to be replanted somewhere else? Lots of times there is still evidence of roots, growing from the sides of the empty hole, severed violently and without consent. From the tree's point of view, if a tree had a point of view, it didn't necessarily want to be moved. It was fine where it was. Then, someone comes along with some heinously sharp tool, rips into the ground and hacks away at the outlying root system, to extricate the tree from its place in the ground. And all that is left is a huge hole, so much bigger than what it seems like should've been left by the missing thing.

That was us. The evidence of my mother was all around. Her family. The beautiful woodwork she restored, the wallpaper she hung, the antiques she scouted out and placed in their positions of honor, the intricately appointed bedrooms of her daughters. She was gone. But we were all left behind living among the severed roots that screamed what used to be. Even then, I felt like it would've been easier to have been the person that died.

I knew I didn't want to be left here to wait for that huge hole to fill in. I didn't think it would be possible, in fact, for that hole to ever be filled in. Living on in a place where nothing changes even though everything has changed is a torture that is difficult to describe. A place where you cannot trust what you see. Everything of potential beauty destroyed and devastated, and yet it all still looked just the same. And so you go on, feeling like your arms and legs have been violently torn from your body, but you're expected to move through each day as if nothing happened.

We weren't allowed to talk about my mom or the loss we all felt so overwhelmingly. Of course, this was never said, but we knew it. We were just supposed to move on. It wasn't like things are now. There was no school counselor or teachers who gave you a little encouragement. There were no friends, or parents of friends, who would acknowledge what had just been stolen from you. No, it seems everyone, *everyone*, was aware of the rule that You Don't Talk About These Things. And so, we didn't talk about the electric pain we were all feeling. We just pretended it wasn't there. After a while, we grew numb to the strength of it, and grew accustomed to its persistent, dull presence.

Once, I answered the phone, and the caller asked for Mrs. Murphy. I couldn't speak. How surreal it was for her to NOT be here, and yet, she certainly wasn't. But, people still called and spoke her name, expected to be connected to her and carry on whatever business they had begun with her.

"She's at work," I managed to get out. My sisters overheard me and howled with laughter. Finally, some levity in this place! But it wasn't funny.

I was given the assignment to clean out Mommy's car, because it was going to be sold. She didn't need it anymore, right? Off it goes. So, out I went to the royal blue Chevy Impala with the white top, the same car we had all piled into for the Myrtle Beach vacation. I gathered trash and swept the floors, emptied the glove box and wiped down the dashboard. And then I found it. An old Kleenex. I picked it up, held it in my hand and wept. This strange souvenir, the only intimate remnant left behind as hard evidence to prove, in my mind, that she had ever been here.

"We've had the evidence analyzed in our secret lab, Bridget, and Francie Murphy's DNA is all over this thing," a CSI might have said.

"AHA! That *proves* she was here. She *was* real!" I would've replied, believing only the evidence and not my sketchy memory.

In the book, *The Secret Life of Bees*,[6] the main character, Lily Owens, has a box of her dead mother's things. She steals out of the house at night to lay outside in the cool darkness, away from her abusive father, to get closer to her momma as she puts on the white gloves once worn by this absent mother. She rests her gloved hands on her bare tummy, a way to connect something that was, to something that is, to prove to herself this person was here once. She wore these gloves. When Lily put the gloves on, her mother and she were connected somehow.

That was what the Kleenex in the car was for me. A peculiar bridge from my living mom to my abandoned, heartbroken soul.

Most of my memories have been vacuum-sealed and roped off, carted away and sequestered for safekeeping, I suppose. I don't remember much about the next years. I was 12 years old, in 7th grade when my mom died. My sister Kellie brings things up from that very dark time, "Don't you remember?" she will ask.

I don't.

Forgetting pain, like a mom who labors for hours to bring forth that precious child she has grown to know over the last 9 months, is merciful. That physical pain is nearly unbearable but what else can you do but move forward in the process and let things take their course. Soon, the pain will be over and a new beginning will be borne. And new fears will proceed after the fear of delivery is over.

"Will I love this child? Will I be able to raise this child? Do I really have what it takes to be a mom?" the new mother may wonder.

I am supposing it is God's mercy that keeps me from remembering the emotional pain of the years that trailed behind my mom's passing. If I could remember details about those years, I would also probably remember, vividly, the terror that each new day brought as the new fear of going on without her replaced the fear of losing her.

"Will I be able to make it through this day? Will I be able to make it through tomorrow and the next day and this life without the love of a mother who loves unconditionally?"

God knows what He is doing. He is faithful to subdue the pain of difficult transitions and seasons. I believe it is His mercy that purged my spirit of the rawness that followed. And, in time, I would come to know another unconditional love.

My childhood home

One of my parents themed parties. This was a gangster party. My dad is on the far right.

My dad (left) and mom (middle) on the Party Porch

The infamous park where Kellie had to clean up all the trash after she chucked the chicken leg over her head.
From far left: Marie, me, Kellie, my mom

The Fat, Frizzy-haired girl the year my mom died.

From left: Shanty, Kellie, MGB, and me

At my graduation from Purdue
From left: Daddy, Marie, me, Kellie and Wayne

Our dogs, Maisie and Buford. Burford's great expectations for peanut butter taught us all how to wait on God.

At my cousin's wedding just 3 months after my mom passed away.

From left: Wayne, Lainey Frances, me and Emmy in 2004

Lainey Frances and me the morning after she gave up her binkies and discovered the Tooth Fairy brought her something better.

Part Two
The Beauty

Chapter 1
The Leader Of The Band

I was a grown woman about to marry my first and only boyfriend. A man that was everything my father wasn't, and nothing that he was. Wayne was calm and kind. Steady. Not a drinker. Not abusive, but loving and adoring. He was quietly tender and funny. With the marriage, I felt *free*!! Free of the oppression of my father and from the grip of the sadness which had come to define who I was.

Even though my career had taken me far from home, we got married in my hometown and were returning to live in the area for a few years, so Wayne could go to graduate school. I was excited to move back home. I looked forward to being near my sisters and my old buddies from high school. I had a good job. Wayne had a great future ahead of him, with a pit stop at graduate school for us to get through. I felt I was returning not as the Fat, Frizzy-haired girl, but as a successful woman who was, in some ways, thumbing her nose at her dear old dad and her old life there.

The wedding had all been planned when we returned late that summer for the beginning of our new life.

Daddy was living with his girlfriend now. Her name was Karen and, at that point, I didn't really know her. I had only met her once, years before, at my college graduation. I had heard her name many times over the years, but I only knew her as "That Karen". I suspect this was Daddy's way of disguising her importance, her relevance, in his life.

"I'm going on a vacation with 'That Karen,'" he might say.

Or, "I was out to dinner with 'That Karen.'"

My dad was an extremely private person, and I have come to believe this was for a couple of reasons. Part of it was generational, most of his peers seemed to me to have been equally as private. Lips were sealed shut about most everything. His privacy was both odd and funny at times. There was actually a time when he drove himself to the emergency room, thinking he was having a heart attack. We found out about it months later, when he uncharacteristically let a few details slip. The other reason I think he operated with so much secrecy was perhaps due to his drinking. He'd had to hide the magnitude of his habit for many, many years. He was accustomed to being very stealth about his personal life. If referring to Karen as "That Karen" made him feel more comfortable, as if he were throwing us off his trail, so be it.

The morning of our wedding, the sky was overcast. It looked to have rained during the night, and I was reassured by my soon-to-be mother-in-law, that if it rained on your wedding day, it was good luck. Okay, I'll take that.

Wayne and I were married at my childhood church.

The one where everything happened! My sisters and I were baptized there. I endured adolescence there. I was an unwilling participant, forced to walk through these doors and keep tabs on who I saw while I was there, so I could prove that I had, indeed, gone to church. (Funny that none of us were held accountable for the message that had been preached, but only to say which of my father's friends we had seen that day, so he could later confer with them to be sure we were telling the truth about being there.) The church my sister and I hid in the coat closet to avoid.

My mother's funeral had been there. I could still clearly hear the children's choir singing from the balcony and smell the thick incense in the air from that day whenever I stepped back into this sanctuary. I definitely felt like the fat, 12-year-old whenever I entered that church.

What's more, this is the church that I felt had let me down so many times during my young life.

This was the church where MGB had a heart attack on Christmas Day while the folks in the sanctuary did nothing to acknowledge or to help us. The mass went on and the priest didn't miss a beat as my dad flew out of the pew, burst through the oversized doors and darted across the busy street outside, knocking on someone's door so he could call an ambulance. Even as the paramedics entered with a stretcher and all their equipment, not a single person glanced our way, but instead, continued reciting the verses, their noses stuck in the missalettes.

No one asking, "Is everything okay? Are you all right?" to which my sisters and I would've said, "NO! We are not all right! Everything is not okay!! Please help us!!!" and it would've been about so much more than

Mean Grandma Betty's heart troubles. But even if they had, Daddy would have shooed them away, citing that it wasn't any of their business.

This was the church where more drama played out when, as a teenager, I came with my sister, Kellie, and asked them to help us to be placed in foster care. Instead of lifting us out of the fear we were soaked in daily, this church had contacted my father and told him we were requesting to be removed from his home, and he better take care of the situation. After all, this would be embarrassing to my dad, and to a certain degree, our church. Words cannot tell you of the fear we had of Daddy when he came home raging and drunk that night, and of the betrayal we felt from our Monseigneur, who had turned us in to the man we were so afraid of.

Despite all of this, I chose to get married there. For me, it was about returning as someone who had triumphed and gotten out whole, more than any deeply positive sentimental attachments to it, because there were none.

Daddy and I rode over in the limo together. He was odd that afternoon, to be sure. But, really, him being odd wasn't really odd. I was so nervous on the ride over, all the moisture in my mouth had leeched out and I could not speak. So, I sat in silence with Daddy, waiting for him to say something profound. I ached for this moment of reconciliation that you always see played out in movies. I had this idea that maybe he would admit that he had made mistakes and hadn't been a good dad. I was hoping he'd tell me he loved me and was proud of me. Don't we all yearn to be accepted and approved by our parents? No matter what the situation, no matter our age. We have an innate need for that. But my movie moment failed to transpire.

"I took a beta blocker back at the hotel. I have more with me, do you want one?" he offered, true to the Medicine Man's character.

Since I was now also in the business of pharmaceuticals, myself, I knew Daddy must have taken this pretty serious blood pressure medicine because it would slow down his heart rate and he wouldn't feel so nervous. I didn't think it was a good idea. But it speaks to how Daddy medicated to override every uncomfortable emotion. Take a pill. Have a drink.

"That's okay. No thanks," I managed.

Pulling up to the church, I was met by my aunt and her daughter. I had invited them secretly. I knew Daddy wouldn't want to see them. And I respected that. But while I knew my dad didn't like my mom's family, for reasons never revealed to me and not truly remembered by him, I couldn't get married without them there. They were all I had left of my mother.

Knowing how Daddy would feel, I tried to make a compromise. I asked them to come to the ceremony, explained forth rightly that Daddy would be angry if he saw them and would they be insulted if I asked them to forgo the reception? They understood and were happy to attend the church service. Never did I foresee that the limo would pull up in front of the church just as they were arriving. Uh-oh. I was busted.

Once downstairs in the church basement, where I had so many years ago, gathered with the rest of the church after mass to eat those pink frosted donuts, and play games at the annual bizarre that my mom had chaired, I waited for it to be time to ascend the stairs and step into the next season of my life. My mom's friends came down to wish me well and provoked the tears that had been waiting to pour out all day. I had a quick cry, with no one knowing quite what to do or say, when the priest came down and said, "It's time."

Waiting in the vestibule to walk me down the aisle, Daddy was pacing like a caged animal. But, I couldn't worry about him right now or about what might be going through his mind.

"He has no power over me anymore," I thought.

The music started, and the doors opened to the sanctuary. Taking the first step into my new life, Daddy got in a few last comments.

"I can't wait to get rid of you," he quietly and clearly snarled through a mouth that did not move, looking straight ahead with a poker face.

"Who cares?" I thought. I could see Wayne at the end of the aisle. I was steps away from leaving all this behind me. The sadness and the fear and the anxiety that had swarmed me for so many, many years, the key origin of that fear and sadness playing out in this exact spot, would be wiped clean as soon as I reached the end of this aisle.

Things got a little weird at the reception when it was time for the father-daughter dance. I had put a lot of thought into the song I would dance to with Daddy. I thought about it for years, really. It was going to be my only way to avenge the wrongs I felt he had perpetrated. I wasn't going to dance with him to the traditional, "Daddy's Little Girl" song. Though he may have wanted that in order to keep up appearances, it was the one thing with him that I got to control. I decided years earlier that, at my wedding, I would dance with him to Dan Fogleberg's *The Leader of the Band*.

It was not, at this point, meant to be hurtful. Rather, it was a way for me to reconcile how my dad had or had not loved us. While it didn't line up perfectly, the lines that spoke to me were:

His hands were meant for different work

And his heart was known to none

He left his home and went his lone and solitary way

And he gave to me a gift I know I never can repay

He earned his love through discipline, a thundering velvet hand

It was mostly the line about how his heart was known to none that spoke to me. That he was solitary and that we earned his love through discipline. I understood the thundering hand of that discipline.

"Will the father of the bride please come to the dance floor?" the disc jockey requested once. Twice. Three times. Awkward. Very awkward.

Daddy, it seems, had been busily pouring whiskey over the wound he sustained when, hours earlier, he saw my aunt back at the church. Manning the bar was his fallback position. He was comfortable and comforted there. To join me on the dance floor for the lore of the father-daughter dance, he had to be extricated from his perch by a few guests.

"Will the Father of the Bride please come to the dance floor?" the disc jockey repeated again. Emerging sourly from the darkened doorway of the bar, I could see Daddy was in a state, to say the least. Maybe it would be better to not have this dance, I remember thinking.

But we got through it, not speaking, just swaying back and forth in a surreal moment.

And that was that!

Upon returning home from our honeymoon, I chose to keep my middle name and let go of my maiden name. Unconventional, I know. But I could do whatever I wanted and so I did. Just like that, I got to drop the Murphy and, all that it meant, out of my life. The injury that it brought with it. I wanted to be free of it. It also didn't hurt that I could give my dad another little, quiet jab, right?

My name wasn't all that changed when Wayne and I returned home. Unbeknownst to me, my fragile relationship with Daddy had changed too, eroding into a new low. Marie called to debrief me on some important events that took place after Wayne and I left our reception. It seems the reception wasn't the only place things got a little weird. Back at the hotel, where most of the wedding guests were staying, Daddy and That Karen had created quite a scene as well. "Daddy was in the hallway, in his underwear, fighting with me and some of the others," Marie delicately tried to tell me. "Then, he locked himself out of his room and he went to the front desk, in his underwear, to get another key."

Honestly, I wasn't sad or embarrassed for him. I was embarrassed for me! What an impression to make on my new family, whom I didn't know very well. All I could picture was Daddy traipsing around the hotel, walking slowly and carefully to keep his balance, in his underwear. Yikes!!

It was also revealed to me that Wayne's mom had seen That Karen early the next morning in the parking lot, wearing her pajamas and stealthily crawling out from the back seat of her car. Apparently, it was quite a bad night for Daddy and That Karen. She had slept in her car.

"He isn't talking to me or Kellie," Marie continued.

Well, that was all it took for me. I was going to see to it that he would talk to me! I was always the one who would confront him. His unaccountability for his actions over the years had caused me to have a very short fuse where I felt injustice was being done. Without thinking, I picked up the phone and within a few seconds, Daddy answered. (Remember, this is pre-caller id!)

"What's going on?" I pounced.

"Nothing," he calmly spoke. "I'm done with all of you."

"Why? What happened?"

Silence.

"Is this really what you want?" I said.

"Yes," he pronounced, sarcastically sweet.

"You're going to die a lonely old man," I hurled, giving him a taste of what it felt like to have to take the impact of someone's words and emotions. These shameful, powerfully hurtful words should never have crossed my lips and I wrestle even now that I ever spoke them. It wasn't right.

"Thank you," he chided.

"Okay. Bye!" I hung up on those words and regretted them immediately. I was always doing that. Confronting without much thought. Relying on sheer emotion and self-righteousness to carry me to the promise of victory over Daddy, or for that matter, anyone who behaved dismissively or unjustly toward me. But victory was never delivered through this erratic behavior of mine. It would be a struggle for me for decades to come.

I know now that I was raw from years of feeling like I didn't matter to the people I was supposed to matter to most. "How dare you treat me like that!!" was my inner battle cry for many, many years. It caused me to lash out in the most benign situations, like, if I thought the cashier at the grocery store was being disrespectful toward me.

This feeling of being dismissed and unvalued caused me to go on the attack that afternoon when I spoke to Daddy. I am not proud. Grace has brought me to the conclusion that this is never the route to justice or healing. But, I didn't know that then.

And so, those were the last words The Leader of the Band and I spoke to each other for about five years.

Daddy was good at this game. This grudge-holding. I was not. Over the years, I tried once, in my abrupt, assaultive way, to reconcile with him. I decided we should just call a truce. I could concede I hadn't been the ideal daughter.

"Let's just start over from here," I thought. So I called him and blurted this out to him when he answered.

Daddy was caught completely off guard, of course. He was not expecting to hear my voice after so much time had passed, and he certainly wasn't going to give up without volleying a few more times.

"No thank you," he had said and softly hung the phone up.

Despite this new family feud, I enjoyed my life as a newlywed. I felt such freedom and lightness as Wayne and I began our life in our ugly, beautiful, cramped apartment with brown shag carpeting, where we lived while Wayne worked on his graduate degree as I excelled in my career.

When Wayne finished his degree, he took a job that required a lot of travel. It gave us the freedom to live wherever we wanted. Since my family was obviously not behaving like the dream family, I was open to moving away again. We found a home and a neighborhood on the east coast that we fell in love with. Well, really, I should say, I found a home and a neighborhood I fell in love with. Wayne wasn't so sure we could afford it, but I pressed and pushed and eventually won.

Looking back, I did a lot of pushing. I see the logic of it now. I felt neglected, like I had no control over life for so long, that I would take things on myself to never feel that way again. Of course, I didn't see it that way at the time. I was just trying to fulfill my dream of having a "Happy Family".

As childish and simplistic as it sounds, that was my greatest desire. In the years after my mom died, as we would be driving somewhere along the flat country roads, I would see these little ranch houses dotting the roadsides here and there, and I would dream of living in one of those simple little houses. I could see myself peeking into my baby's nursery, cooking dinner and waiting for my Prince Charming husband to come home from work. It was a day dream that served to comfort me and drive me forward to attain it.

This house was the "Happily Ever After" house I had dreamed of! I knew it! Wayne was hesitant, because we would be short on cash, with only one income, as I was leaving the corporate world and taking my turn in graduate school. But in the end, Wayne came around and we did have quite a sweet fairy tale going. It was at the Happily Ever After house that I got the peculiar, unexpected letter from Daddy. The salutation, itself, was odd. It started out like this:

"Dear Bridget, Kellie and Marie (alphabetical order):"

What a strange way to begin a letter, but that's what it said.

Daddy was easily offended and supremely suspicious, so he assumed we were also looking to be offended. It was for this reason he made sure we knew he addressed us in no order of favoritism, but simply alphabetically.

As if we might be saying, "Wait! Why was your name first and not mine?"

My sisters and I could picture him and That Karen sitting around cussing and discussing, in their shared alcohol-induced paranoia, about the best way to address those brats of his. "Maybe in order of birth?" he would offer.

"NO! They'll think you're favoring Marie," That Karen may have answered.

"Hey! I've got it! Let's just do it in alphabetical order, that way no one can accuse me of anything," he must have finally settled on.

Yes, because it's normal and healthy to devote that

much time and thought to the order of names on a letter.

Seeing our names that way reminded me of when Daddy paid Kellie and me for doing some yard work with money from the Almighty Change Jar in his room, the one I regularly raided for lunch money. He called us his into room and instructed us to hold our hands out. In them, he placed exactly $2 each, in various configurations. And then he said, "Even Steven. Even Steven."

Kellie and I had not known what he was talking about. Later, we realized he thought we may compare our change and think that, since we didn't have the exact same coinage, we would riot, believing one of us had been shortchanged (pun intended). His suspicious mind led him to reassure us: the fruits of our labor were evenly paid. Okay.

So the salutation on the letter was a bit like a declaration of "Even Steven". As if, after what we read in the letter, we would care what order our names had been listed in.

The letter explained, very coldly, how Daddy and That Karen had quietly gotten married a few months back and were just now letting us know. The wedding date for the happy couple? December 13th. They had gotten married, you see, on the anniversary of my mother's death. Not that I am now or ever was a freak about such things, but it hurt. It felt disrespectful, dishonorable, both to my mom and to her daughters. It went on to say my dad decided to get married on that day so he could "redeem the date" for himself. I felt my sisters and I were disregarded, again, as legitimate participants in the family, just as we had been all those years ago, while my mother was actively dying. Bystanders, who had no stake in things.

This was the part that bothered me about the way the wedding went down. He'd wanted to let us know we didn't matter to him or belong to him, and so he owed us nothing more than this strange memo we received.

To me, it was reinforcement of my status as an orphan. After my mom died, I felt like an orphan, even though my dad was still living. He was so detached from us; it wasn't a stretch to think of myself as a stray child. I had a longing for belonging, an awareness of an emptiness, that seemed impossible to assuage. I have come to know it's the heart that alerts us to orphan status, not necessarily the legality of our situation.

"Fine with me. If that's how he wants it, I can forget about him as easily as he forgot about us," I rationalized. But when I found out I was pregnant, I had a feeling of panic. I wanted my child to know her grandfather. It was hard enough that my mom wouldn't know me as a mom or know my children. I wanted my dad involved. I wanted that belonging both for my child and for myself.

Knowing how my phone call had been so badly received years earlier, I decided to send a letter of my own. It was short and to the point. I explained I was pregnant, and would very much like for him to be a part of my and my child's life. Knowing what I know now, I see the walls and harshness Daddy put up were to protect himself, not to shut us out. This baby we were waiting for presented Daddy and I both with a way to start over, do things differently.

It was here, at this place, where things started to "heal" for my dad and me. I say heal but what I mean is that we decided to move on. Nothing was ever talked about. And that was how Daddy needed it to be. For me, I needed to discuss the pink elephant in the room. It's so hard for me to walk over ground that has been decimated and pretend that there is wholeness where there is obvious devastation - that hole with the once living thing ripped out - let's just pretend that hole isn't there.

What hole?

Exactly.

But that was the only path I had with Daddy, and so I chose to pursue it his way. A few weeks later, I received a package containing an embroidered quilt that had clearly belonged to one of us girls. It was Daddy's way of saying, "Okay."

It wasn't a deep relationship we put together after that, but it was relatively stable. He was the first phone call we made after Lainey Frances was born.

I wanted to name her after my mom, but felt that saddling her with the name Frances wasn't fair or kind. These old-fashioned names are very popular now, but at the time, it just seemed like it was cruel. So, we put my momma's name in the middle. I knew girls who were called by their first and middle names. Mary Katherine or Mary Pat. It appealed to me. Like, they were loved so much, they got two names. They were worth the effort of speaking both names. I liked this idea and, even now, make it a point to call her not just Lainey, but Lainey Frances. I don't think she digs it.

So, Daddy and I were renewed in this tenuous way. He loved Lainey Frances with a vulnerability I had never seen him show. We visited several times over the next few years. But, during this time of reunion, Daddy became ill. He developed shingles, just a few years before the vaccine became available.

When That Karen... should I drop "That" now, since we have come to the point in the story where they are married and no longer secretly conducting their relationship? Okay, deal.

When Karen called to tell us that Daddy had this condition, we didn't think it was anything to be too concerned about. Shingles are painful, but not life threatening and typically, not long-lasting.

We began praying for Daddy and would tell Lainey Frances, "Let's pray for Grandpa. He doesn't feel good." And so, that became part of our nightly routine with her.

But the shingles didn't go away. A year and a half passed and he still had the unbearable pain they brought. It kept him from living his life. It kept him from many trips we planned. Daddy and Karen were going to visit us for Lainey Frances's 3rd birthday, but were afraid they would have to cancel. As I put Lainey to bed one night just before their anticipated arrival, I said, "Okay, sweetie, let's pray for God to make Grandpa better."

She twisted her head and looked up at me, "He not make him feel better yet?!" she asked incredulously.

Daddy and Karen did make it out for that trip and we were blessed to have that time together. I was so happy that Daddy got to come to my home and know me, not as the Fat, Frizzy-haired girl he made to stand in a field while he thought of cruel names to call me, all in "good, clean fun", but as a good mom, homemaker, and wife, who had grown up well, despite both of our failures, mistakes, and shortcomings!

But Daddy was in a lot of pain and had lost a lot of

weight. He slept a great deal of the time he was at my house. He was clearly not doing well. His health was deteriorating, not improving.

When they visited after my second daughter, Emelia Ruth, was born, Daddy looked even worse. Enduring the intense, chronic physical pain was weakening his immune system. The medicine they gave him to control the pain made him not just sleepy, but scary sleepy. He would be sitting upright in a chair, his head lolled over to one side, passed out with his eyes open and rolling slightly back in his head.

Passing by him this way, I was overcome with terror. I thought he had died in the chair. Fear seized my throat so that I couldn't speak. My heart pounding out of my chest, I got Karen and coaxed her, speechless, to come with me so I could show her my gruesome discovery.

She actually laughed, "The medicine does that to him. He's okay."

At some point after that, they began putting tape over his eyes so that he wasn't so frightening to potential passersby. Sleeping with your eyes open isn't just creepy, it's also painful, so the hope was that taping his eyes shut would prevent them from drying out.

This was the first of many accommodations that were made for the strange little problems that came with his growing list of conditions. To help with the painful neuropathy in his hands, he began to wear golfing gloves because the pressure of the adjustable glove alleviated some of his pain.

He told me once, "I'm pretty scary looking in my full regalia." At least he could appreciate a little humor in this.

That summer we decided to go to Daddy's and spend a few weeks at the lake with him. So as not to disturb him, we rented the lake house next to theirs, as these folks were typically only there a few weeks of the year and were happy to make some rental income. It was a great vacation. Daddy got to spend some amazing time not only with his daughters, but also with his granddaughters.

There was a lot going on about this time. Kellie was engaged to be married and we were having a bridal shower for her. It was good. It was normal. It was happy! But Daddy was still sick and had gotten much worse. We could see that he was losing a lot of weight.

He wasn't just the scary sleeper anymore. He was also the incredibly shrinking man. I was alarmed when I saw him so thin. But he and Karen assured us that it was just the shingles causing his heartburn to kick up. As soon as those darn shingles were gone, they guaranteed us, his heartburn would ease and he would be able to eat and be robust again.

Hmmmmm....it didn't sound right to me. He'd had shingles for more than two years at that point. My sisters and I thought there had to be something else going on. But we went along with his story because that was what he wanted. He had flat-out said, "I don't have cancer. The doctors ruled that out." Because, of course, we had all seen cancer ravage a body, firsthand. After you've watched someone carried off by cancer, or you've had cancer yourself, I think that fear is always right there for you. It's always what you think of first and it can make your heart beat out of your chest until you get the all clear. This was all looking very familiar.

Just before we left from that visit, Daddy fell on the deck one night. He insisted it was because he had low blood pressure. Marie and Karen struggled to get him into a chair and stabilize him.

After seeing the most highly-regarded doctors in the state, Daddy decided he was going to make a pilgrimage to a very well-known, highly-respected hospital to get a diagnosis once and for all. We were thrilled. More than anything, I wanted to be able to enjoy our newly established truce, to have that "Happy Family" that had become an idol to me.

I felt like I should go with them on this pilgrimage. I wasn't confident we had the whole story. But, I had this new, sweet little baby who was prone to being sick and who couldn't keep much down herself. Her pediatrician assured me this was just reflux and was no great cause for alarm. All babies spit up, she explained.

Well, I wouldn't exactly call this spitting up. Emmy would projectile vomit at least once a day, often more than once. And when she did, it was as if someone literally poured a few hefty gallons of goo down on all of us. Poor Emmy would have it all over herself. It soaked whoever was feeding her. It daily covered a good part of the kitchen floor, sometimes even going into the adjacent family room. It wasn't just a quick clean up. Anyone near the scene had to be stripped, possibly bathed, and the debris cleaned up from the floor, the walls, the table, sometimes the dog!

She was also prone to what we thought were ear infections. We have since been told that more than likely,

Emmy's stomach acid was backing up into her Eustachian tubes, because they weren't completely formed yet, which is why giving her round after round of antibiotics never worked. It wasn't a problem of an infection. It was a problem of having fluid where it didn't belong and it caused her to be crying in pain a lot.

But, all of that was discovered years down the road. At the time, we just thought she had frequent, powerful ear infections that defied antibiotic treatment. And so, with this new baby seeming so fragile to me, I was hesitant to leave her. Of course, I knew Wayne would take wonderful care of her, but as any mother knows, it is so very, very difficult to leave a sick child. But, I did leave Wayne and the girls, and set off one beautiful September evening to go to the series of doctor visits which were lined up to diagnose the ugliness that had made its way into our world.

Chapter 2

Recognition

Now, I must interrupt the story here and step back for an important newsflash! There was a time in the year after Lainey Frances was born that I had a full-on encounter with God. It was quite unexpected on my part, certainly not something I was actively seeking.

I had heard people say they knew God. How? People told me they heard God speak to them. Really? People told me they trusted God. Why? People said God was good. Sometimes, maybe.

Knowing God reminded me of the Mission Impossible series, (the television series from the '70s, of course, not the Tom Cruise movies). At the beginning of every episode, there was an assignment given to the secret agents. It would be dangerous and difficult and, well, darn near impossible. But, if they chose to accept the top-secret assignment, they would be in for quite an adventure.

Maybe, like one of those spies, it was my job in life to uncover God's goodness and find His Presence in those past events, to wrestle His blessing away from Him. But I simply wasn't interested.

In my mind, He didn't want to be known, or heard, just blindly and ignorantly trusted.

Here's the thing, up to this point in my life, I already knew everything I needed to know about God. I was not inclined to trust Him. I hadn't wanted to go digging for evidence of Him or His alleged goodness. I'd already learned to deal with the Gotcha God. With solid fear and complete avoidance! Therefore, I had absolutely no desire to take on the impossible mission of finding Him.

The funny thing is, as I see now, He came looking for me!

I met some women who casually invited me to a Bible study. I went, because I was in hot pursuit of, you guessed it, friends! But I was more than a little uncomfortable with the invitation. People like me didn't go to Bible studies. People like me didn't even own a Bible.

At the end of the first meeting, these ladies prayed. And they prayed, in my mind, about silly things. Things you don't go bugging God about. Like, one of them prayed for her baby to sleep through the night.

Wait. Whaaaaat? You can't do that. You can't pray for your kids to sleep. These must be some of those "Jesus freaks" my dad had warned me about! One of them even began to cry as she shared a personal story about "how God was a father" for her.

"Okay, first of all," I critiqued internally, "God doesn't care about whether your kid sleeps or not. He doesn't really care about any of us much. And, second, don't even get me started on the whole 'God as a father' thing!" The majority of my experience with "fatherly" love looked volatile, frightening, questionable, and unreliable.

True, this "caring God" sure looked good on these ladies, but I doubted it would work for me. The Fat, Frizzy-haired girl hadn't made it onto this team, I already knew that.

Except I had to admit, seeing what those ladies had, it made me momentarily rethink my opinion of God. If God was truly like they seemed to think He was, maybe, I would be willing to give Him a chance.

With this decision, I must've opened the door, just a crack.

I was driving my first real Grown Up Car, the paprika-colored Taurus that we called the "Winnie the Pooh" mobile because, it was all "Winnie-ed" out!

There was the window shade with Winnie, skipping happily across it, the Winnie the Pooh toys that were attached to the car seat, and, of course, the Winnie the Pooh music that was always playing to quiet the baby in back who tended to get carsick. Cruising down the country road, listening to the roll call of who lived in the Hundred Acre Woods, I had been satisfied with the accommodations I had made for myself to deal with life apart from God.

Here comes the "all of a sudden" moment: All of a sudden, a deer popped out of the tall grassy field just to my right. The beast was in the middle of a big and powerful leap to the street.

"I'm going to hit that deer," I calmly acknowledged in my mind.

With nowhere for me to go on the narrow Pennsylvania road, I was resigned to the collision. I mentally went through an abbreviated check list in the split-second I had before the deer completed its dive out in front of the Winnie-the-Pooh car.

"Lainey is strapped in - she'll be fine. If that animal doesn't come through the windshield, we'll be okay."

Slamming on the breaks, I braced myself for the impact.

But there was no impact.

At the edge of the road, the deer was hanging, inexplicably, in the air. It hadn't finished its leap into the road, but was pulled back, mid-arc. On its hind legs, it stood up like a dog begging for a treat. It hung like that for a second, then, dropped to all four legs and was gone.

This is when I heard God.

"That was me," I heard quietly inside.

And it was over. No swerving, out of control car. No deer. No deer carcass.

It was only natural to think, "Did that really just happen?"

It seemed surreal. But I knew I had seen that deer jumping. I knew it wasn't natural for a deer to be hiked up in the air like that. And I knew I'd heard that voice. I recognized it was God, because I recognized it wasn't me. I knew enough about the Bible to know God's voice is described as "still and small". And that fit. That was the way I heard Him.

There went my theory that God didn't speak to the average person, because He had just spoken to me. True, He hadn't spoken through a typical miracle, if there is such a thing. No burning bush or pillar of fire. But, my experience with the deer *was* miraculous. I knew that deer was literally held back, and held up, long enough for me to see it.

I could easily have missed or dismissed it. But the stamp of God, even though I had never seen Him before, was all over the moment.

I also knew that Jesus described His followers as sheep, who recognized His voice.

And I had just recognized Him.

Hmmmmm...maybe. Maybe I was one of His sheep.

The next time I heard from God, I was down in the primitive, dimly lit basement where my hard-working washer and dryer lived. The house was quiet, now with two daughters napping, and I was alone with my thoughts - a place I never liked to be.

Wrestling with the wet, tangled sheets coming out of the washer and stuffing them into the dryer, I was performing the same actions with my thoughts - wrestling and stuffing. The same contenders, predictably, showed up for me to grapple with in these quiet moments when nothing in particular was going through my mind.

Ever since the deer, I wanted to keep alive the God who was good and cared enough about me to hold up the deer like a trophy, a big fish on a fishing line, as if to say, "See what I did for you?" I wanted to keep seeing that good God who cared about the details of my day. I wanted to be brought to tears, too, when I told people who He was. I was actively looking to keep finding that God. But still, I had this obstacle that I couldn't get around.

"If You are good, and You love me, why did You let my mother die?"

No answer for that one? "I'm sorry God, but this one is kind of a deal breaker for me. I don't understand."

By now, the grip the enemy had on me with this question had grown, mutated, and metastasized. Now, not only was I grieving my mother, I was mourning the absence of her presence as my daughters' grandmother. More chilling, however, I was also a mother who was anticipating that any day, I would be diagnosed with breast cancer, myself, and my own daughters would be doomed to grow up motherless.

And in this every day ordinary chore of doing laundry, God bent down, again, to speak to me.

"Her journey is not your journey," the quiet whispered to me.

"What? Is that you?"

Silence.

"But why did you let her die?"

"Her journey is not your journey," I heard deeply.

It's something I would equate to a download. Hearing happened in a flash, but so much more was imparted than was made known in that instant. "Files" were left to be poured over, even after the moment passed.

From those files, I got a picture of two circles in my mind. One was my mom's and one was mine. My circle didn't lay on top of her circle, nor did it overlap at all. It was next to hers, the edges just touching in a small spot.

"But what about her?" I insisted, wondering why she had to go. Was she okay? Was she in heaven? Was she sad?

Silence.

In the dark, waiting to hear more, desperate to hear more, nothing else was spoken to me. But something was given to me. A slice of peace was doled out to me in the basement that day. Before I even finished pulling out the sheets, I was aware that a sliver of the grief I carried with me, and acknowledged almost daily, had eased slightly. It wasn't a lightning bolt moment. But, I perceived an easing of the heaviness I had gotten used to toting around.

More pouring through the files. Her journey was her journey. I filled in the blanks.

Her journey was between her and God. It wasn't mine to ponder or carry or figure out. God surely had good reason for taking her.

If God met up with me here in my laundry room to talk about this twenty year-old issue, then I decided I was going to accept His somewhat cryptic answer and the clarity it brought with it. Instead of trying on the "what ifs", I decided I was going to pick up and put on the peace I felt coming from Him. From that experience, whenever the scary thought of being eaten up with breast cancer invaded my mind, I remembered my basement moment.

"Her journey is not your journey."

Any time I remembered my close encounter with God in the basement, I felt *clothed* in that same peace and stillness. And it was mine whenever I called on it.

With these two encounters, I could concede that maybe we could just skip the "What about my mom" question *for a while*. I wasn't letting Him "off the hook" about my mom. But, at least we were talking now. Since I had begun spending time getting to know God through the Bible, I could compare my unanswered question to when Peter asked Jesus what was going to become of the disciple, John. He hadn't gotten an answer either. So, I accepted that if Peter didn't get an answer, it was okay if I didn't get one, for now, too.

"I get it, God. You want to talk to me about *me*, not my mom. Her journey is not my journey."

And since her journey was not my journey, I regarded it as a promise that I was not going to repeat her journey. I was not going to get breast cancer.

Then, I had my first abnormal mammogram. They called me to report that I had an "undefinable mass." Now, this topic of my many abnormal mammograms could be a book, itself, but I will cut to the chase for the sake of making my point.

I went through that struggle with the first breast cancer scare, and I came out of it with the gift of *peace*.

Of course, initially, I was an absolute mess. After I had a few hours to digest the news, I was alone in my car, and had a screaming melt down in the privacy and safety it afforded me.

"You promised!" I shrieked. I beat my fists furiously on the steering wheel and pounded my feet in unbridled anger.

"You promised!" I screamed, leaving my throat raw

for days.

Driving to get the follow-up MRI that had been ordered, I was listening to a Christian CD, trying to hang onto the hope and promise I thought I had. The song by Philips, Craig and Dean called, "You are Good" proclaimed that God was good and His love endures.

Through tears, I listened and thought, "Wait, I need to remember this. You *are* good. You have been good to me." And this calmed me down.

God was *good*. He had shown me that by coming to talk to me, personally. That was proof that He cared, that He was good. Everything had turned out good for me, and right now, it was still okay.

Since the laundry room encounter, I'd made a habit of thinking about the goodness of Him bending to meet me in my day to day life. Like testing a frozen pond to see if it was safe to venture out and skate upon, I would wake up each day and test that peace. Is it still there? Is it safe to go through my day, trusting that God's voice is recognizable, that He is real, and that I can truly know Him?

It had remained real and true for me. Rather than putting on the old, familiar garments of despair and sadness, I had actively chosen to put on the peace I got from those memories of the deer and the laundry room. And it had felt good. The peace I received was real and it had held for me. But what about now, with this development? Was it going to hold now?

Just as He had before, God came to me again. In the turmoil I was feeling, He spoke.

"Even if you die, I am still good. I will take care of

your daughters."

His words may seem cold. But I didn't receive them that way. True, they were certainly not the words I wanted to hear. I wanted to have the sense of being reassured that I didn't have the dreaded disease in my body. But He gave me a different kind of reassurance.

Like a parent takes their child's chin, looks them softly in the eyes and gently explains a difficult reality to their young one, this is what God did for me that day

"But I don't want them to go through what I went through!!" I countered back. The download came when I stopped with all my, "Yes, but..." interjections.

He *had* taken care of me. He had brought me up and out of that dark, violent, gaping hole. He had restored me. No, I didn't get to have a mom. But, I got to *be* one! And it was good. And He is good. And His goodness holds. And I can trust Him to take care of my own daughters.

The reassurance, for me, wasn't in the message, but that He was *present* to speak the message. Because I'd absolutely not wanted to hear: *"Even if you die, I am still good."* The peace came, despite His undesirable disclosure, *because* He had spoken. For me, it was confirmation of the sureness and responsiveness of His Presence with me. He was there.

Still, I wanted to press God, saying, "You promised this wouldn't happen to me." But, He hadn't promised that, had He? I had presumed it. Another download: Did my peace come from me thinking I had His promise that I wouldn't get cancer or did that peace come from *knowing* Him?

Knowing He is good and His love endures? *Trusting* that no matter what things look like, He works all things together for good? Trusting, I have found, is an ongoing journey, not an event.

He *was* promising to take care of my little girls. And right then, that was enough.

With this latest bending of the Almighty to me, I saw that I did *know* Him. That He could tell me what should seem like bad news, and yet I received comfort from it, gave me a fuller picture of Him. He was not militant and unapproachable. He was soft and living and responsive. He was right there in my car with me, and spoke to me first through the song, and then straight to my heart.

All of that was given to me in that one little interaction with Him.

The download even reached back to the time after my mom died, when I felt so alone. I didn't think God was good or that His love was enduring back then. What I had understood then was the fear of God. Acutely aware that I ought to stay scared of this unpredictable, unknowable deity, I felt God had always restrained Himself from smiting his billions of unruly children.

What I comprehended in this moment, though, was even though I didn't acknowledge His Presence with me all those years ago doesn't mean He wasn't there. If He was speaking to me in my ordinary moments now, chances are He had been speaking then, too. I just hadn't heard Him or even thought to look for Him.

He must've been there, taking care of me, though I hadn't recognized Him. So, He would be there for my daughters, no matter what twists and turns my own journey took.

It was then that I went from feeling like one of a jillion of his unruly, barely-tolerated children, to an *only* child who was fiercely loved, patiently waited for and tenderly spoken to. Thankfully, it was with this revelation of who my Heavenly Father was that I pressed into the journey of my dad's illness.

Chapter 3
The Leader of the Band

Knocking softly on Daddy and Karen's door at the hotel, I was uneasy. For many reasons. I didn't know what to expect when I saw him. The last time I'd seen him was about 2 months prior, when he had fallen on the deck and they rationalized that it was low blood sugar.

I was also uneasy, because, in these few years since we had delicately reconciled, I had never been alone with the two of them. I always had my family around, to sort of distract from the burden of our past, nobody knowing quite what to do with it. We'd never had to address it before, because the opportunity was never available. But, here, it would just be the three of us. I may have time with my dad now to close all that past, if indeed, that was what should be done.

I was also feeling concerned about Daddy's salvation. When he died, and that was looking imminent the last time I saw him, would he be with God, in His Kingdom? Not to beat an ailing horse, but I have explained the kind of "believers" we were. Believers who thought that if we were good enough, and did all the right things, we may, just maybe, be allowed to be citizens of heaven. But you see, that was all based on what *we* did or didn't do. I'd never understood that my salvation was based solely on what Jesus already did on the cross. That there was nothing I could add to the work He already did. My part was, and is, only to believe, to acknowledge that the price for my sin had already been paid by my Savior, Jesus Christ.

Did Daddy know that? I felt pressed to impart my revelation on him during this trip. But, it wasn't something I wanted to do or even knew how to do. Daddy had always said his relationship with God was "personal" and he didn't want to talk about it. In his way of looking at it, if you were one of those "born agains," you were a nut job!

Once, when Marie presented a necklace to Lainey with a cross on it, she told Lainey, "I'm giving you this cross to remind you that Jesus died for you on a cross so you can to go to heaven someday."

Well, she may as well have been a tambourine-banging, Hari Krishna, gown-wearing freak passing out carnations at the airport. Daddy sucked in his breath through his tightly set mouth and made the sounds that let us all know he thought Marie was "out there".

So, me sharing my new revelation of the gospel, the good news that we can simply take hold of what Jesus already accomplished, this was not going to be easy. Daddy had not shown himself to be receptive to conversations about Jesus.

The quiet in the hallway was interrupted by the click of the lock on the other side of the door. Karen looked tired, but happy to see me. Both she and Daddy tried hard to deny the weight of why we were all there, and what it could mean. We were finally going to get an answer as to why Daddy was losing so much weight, and, why he could not eat, no matter how much he wanted to swallow the food his body was dying to get.

They acted as though we were going to see a football game the next day, and we were getting an early start on tailgating. Daddy played bartender and poured drinks for all of us. But of course, he couldn't have a drink, because it wasn't just food Daddy couldn't swallow. He was unable to swallow the amber liquid that had dulled his pain for most of his life. It was not an option for him any longer. Nor were the cigarettes that also brought him comfort and solace and, in some way, joy. If he could have had a drink or smoked, I am certain he would have. Recall that even my mother continued to smoke and drink after her diagnosis.

"She's already got cancer," Daddy would defend her to horrified onlookers. "What else can happen?"

But, Daddy's illness wouldn't permit him to take solace from these old friends. He physically could not.

They sat with me as I told them about my trip, that I thought I had seen one of the NFL coaches downstairs in the elevator. We caught up for a little while and went to bed. Laying on the pull-out couch that the suite offered, I couldn't sleep. What would we find out tomorrow? Daddy had been there a few days when I arrived and had a lot of tests done already. We'd know the results of these tests tomorrow. Daddy and Karen seemed full of hope. I was not. I knew this was not going to be as simple as they were hoping. Maybe they knew that too, and chose to look beyond the obvious and believe the best, hanging onto the notion that there was hope, for however long they could. If that were the case, I understood that, too.

The famous hospital was quite an impressive place. It proved to be a well-oiled machine, diagnosing patients and aggressively treating them with any number of experimental drugs because of the clinical trials they are involved in. A medical wonderland where the "next thing" is always available and waiting to be tried. Their team approach was all-encompassing and painstakingly scheduled for us.

Daddy would be seeing not one, not two, not even three doctors that day, but so many that I can't accurately recall who they were or what their specialties were. The idea is, instead of seeing, say, the oncologist one day and having to wait a week to see the gastroenterologist the next week to see what she thought about the prescribed course of treatment, you go from doctor to doctor in a day or two, and those doctors are all talking with one another, so there are no vague opinions or thoughts from one practitioner to the next.

In the lobby of the clinic, I sunk heavily into my seat as we waited to begin our marathon of appointments for the day. Weighed down in that chair, I wanted to stay there and not get up. Let's just sit here and pretend nothing else is going on. But the voice of the Spirit was steady in my spirit.

"It's time," it seemed to be saying. I needed to be sure, so I waited, reluctantly, not wanting to be too forward, feeling like I would be accosting Daddy with my beliefs and concerns for his eternity. But that was just my fear. This was no time to worry about stepping on toes. God was telling me - impressing on me - the urgency of my testimony to my dad.

I got up and sat down awkwardly next to him.

"Can I pray with you before we go in?" I asked, hoping to sound casual but my heart was pounding.

"Okay," he answered meekly, so unlike him.

Accustomed to the scripted prayers we had always said, Daddy was not expecting my "free form" prayer. But I didn't hear any protests from him. I don't know what I said. I rambled. Sometimes the enemy will even bring up this bungled moment in my mind, berating me: "Oh that was really good. You blew it."

But, I can give that voice no weight. In that moment with my dad, there in the gravity of what was about to happen, I relied upon the Spirit to speak through me in a way that would reach my weak and small Daddy. I do remember, at the end of my prayer, I asked God to please "take care of this wonderful man." These words evoked a sound of disbelief and surprise from Daddy. This was none of the things I'd rehearsed saying to him, all those years of mentally giving him the verbal lashing I thought he deserved. It just rolled off my tongue, like water running through the fingers of a loosely cupped hand.

I recognize, now, that those were words of forgiveness to Daddy's ears. Even if I wasn't sure I meant the words that tumbled out, I knew they were healing to him then, and they became balm for me in later years.

The relief I felt once I could check that prayer off my list was short-lived, because we were called back soon after, to begin the litany of proclamations from the doctors.

Equipped with a small notebook, I was ready to take notes on exactly what the doctors were saying. Karen had mentioned to me on the phone once, that when she took my dad to his various appointments, she usually felt clear on what the doctors said - until she walked out the door. Then she and my dad would consult one another saying: "What did he say about *abc*?" "We should have asked *xyz*."

I wanted to write down exactly what was spoken, because my sisters and I knew Karen and Daddy were not relaying all that was being said about his condition. It was important for me to get an accurate picture of what the prognosis really was, so that we could prepare, emotionally - my sisters and me. We already experienced our mom dying without being told that was even a possibility. That was the equivalent of a head-on collision into a concrete wall, no warning and no rebound. Just a sickening crash with no softness to be found.

Marie and Kellie and I, even though we never communicated this to one another, didn't want to be caught so off guard again. We wanted time to speak and act and mend with Daddy, even if he didn't want to. For that, we needed some time to think things through. By taking detailed notes, I would be able to look them over later, in a room with air left in it, and decipher what was truly happening. Because, just like with my mom, it was hard to think logically about my dad. But, this time, I knew things could happen, though unimaginable. And, looking at Daddy, it may have been unthinkable but it was not unimaginable. Like Mommy on the "party porch", returning from the hospital, he looked skeletal as he shuffled into the first office.

Once, when I was in college, I saw a girl I knew from home walking down the street toward me. Our parents had been friends in our former life, when my mom was still alive. Like most of the "extra" people in our lives, they dropped off after Mommy died. But I remembered hearing that this daughter of theirs had been hospitalized a few times for anorexia. It was horrifyingly clear she was still suffering from the consuming illness.

Her hair had looked like a small array of straw, dead and lifeless, on her head. Her long arms, dangling at her sides, looked like the hinged arms on a "festive" Halloween skeleton, long and thin and exaggerated. The joints in her elbows and wrists captured my attention, because they had the appearance of being supersized by the smallness of the rest of her frame. The joints at her wrists looked, proportionally-speaking, like golf balls that had been somehow affixed to the sides of her bones. Her face was hollow and her eyes sunken and dark. Like Daddy, her stride wasn't normal, but accomplished with great effort and jerkiness.

Folded into a chair in the cramped office, Daddy looked small and weak. Where was the man who had terrified me all those years? He was not here. His own body had consumed itself as it was starved for food. He was a fraction of what he had been.

The unspoken that day was louder than the spoken.

Yes, we finally got a name for Daddy's illness. The diagnosis? Esophageal cancer with metastasis to the liver and bones. It was a death sentence.

Would it be a quiet slipping away? Hardly. It had already dragged us through the barbed and spiked days of the last few years. The book *War Horse*[7] flashed in my mind's eye - soldiers in trenches, barbed wire, bombs, and lethal gases being hurled. Some of the soldiers would be fortunate enough to die instantly. Others would be left to endure the sheer agony of a slow and sure leaking away of life, the muddy trenches paradoxically giving them refuge but also imprisoning them.

Daddy's whole life had been a battle and here he was, the unfortunate soldier, who was apparently going to be left in the forsaken, hopeless trench, which was his own body, waiting for death to come and relieve him of his life.

We were suspended in the hard reality of the doctor's words for a moment. What do you say after that? "Thank you. We'll just let ourselves out?"

Daddy spoke first. Quietly, calmly, confidently, the Medicine Man volunteered himself for a clinical trial. Having worked all his life in the pharmaceutical industry, he was knowledgeable about the process of these trials, and that they were bastions of hope for those allowed to participate. It was the card he had up his sleeve. It was why he could remain calm during this debriefing we were in.

"No, you're not a candidate," the doctor responded bluntly.

A long look from Daddy. "Okay, well, if something comes up, I would like to be considered."

True, his voice sounded sure and steady, but in it I could hear desperation. I felt that desperation.

"Mr. Murphy, you are not a good candidate. I think you should concentrate on going home and getting things in order."

I focused on my notes, not looking up, but instead, stealing glances at the stranger in the chair across the room, unable to process how this giant in my life could be so diminished with just a few sentences.

I couldn't bear to look at him. He tried to look as though he wasn't fazed. To me, it was like watching a fish that's been left on a pier, its gills moving slowly, no longer thrashing about, morosely confident in the outcome. This was far harder to watch than if he'd shown some emotion. The calm exterior did not comfort me. I knew inside, he was thrashing.

Later, I felt sorry for the doctor, too. I thought about how hard it must've been for him to deliver news of this caliber to three hopeful faces. Daddy was young still, only in his 60's, and prior to having shingles, had led an active life of traveling and spending time with friends. Had the doctor paused outside the door to collect himself before he came in? Had he broken down amongst his peers? Because this wasn't just a cancer diagnosis. It was a sentencing to the agonizing death of deprivation that came with esophageal cancer, the victim eventually dying of starvation, prolonged by the liquid supplements being delivered through a port in the stomach. Like throwing buckets of water on that fish, drawing out the inevitable, instead of just letting the poor creature die expediently.

"No," the next doctor quietly shook his head. "There are no new drugs in the pipeline."

"No, there is no surgery we can do to remove the cancer," another confirmed.

In office after office, doctor after doctor, each shook his or her head as Daddy's quiet request for a spot in a clinical trial was methodically met with a quiet, unyielding "no". The reserved and sure responses we got that day weren't conveyed cruelly, just definitely. There was no dickering around with "maybe".

Like, "Maybe if we can get some weight on you, you would qualify as a good risk for this or that trial." It has been my experience that doctors like to give some scenario of maybe. It makes their job, in that moment, easier. They don't have to be in the room with a dead man walking. They can make it a room with a possible reprieve. But not that day. Not for Daddy.

"Please God, let him have something! Some hope! Something!" I did my own pleading. "We were just getting things together with him. Please let Daddy have the chance to be a grandfather! Please let us have this! Please!"

But I heard nothing in response.

"We'll try to make you as comfortable as possible...."

But they never finished the sentence. The whole thought would have been this: "We'll try to make you as comfortable as possible until you die."

To achieve this "comfort" it was decided that the doctors would do a procedure where a stint was inserted into his esophagus. This would spread open the esophagus, effectively pushing the tumor out of the way, so that food could pass through and Daddy could eat, while he waited for death to come.

We all headed back to the hotel that night feeling that we had some small conquest over the cancer. At last and, at least, he would be able to eat. But this victory did not hold.

Within minutes of the doctors taking Daddy to the procedure room the next morning, Karen and I were summoned.

"Wait a minute," I thought. "We shouldn't be back there. This is bad."

The long walk into the cold and cavernous space, where Daddy lay at the far end, looking so small in the vastness of the room, slammed me back to the long walk I took to see my mom at the funeral home. These two life-altering walks had gruesome similarities and unacceptable endings. Dwarfed, dead or dying parents on the other side.

"Ma'am, your husband's tumor is not blocking his esophagus." The doctor explained. "This is extremely rare, but his tumor is actually on the *outside* of the esophagus and is holding it open permanently. There is no way to close or narrow the opening, and so stomach acid is constantly being brought up and is causing him a lot of pain. Does this make sense?"

Yes, Karen nodded, it did make sense.

Our last ray of hope for some comfort was now gone.

"Okay. We are not going to be able to do this procedure today. I'm sorry. Do you understand what we're saying, Mr. Murphy?"

Yes, Daddy conceded. He spoke like he was the one in charge. Like it was somebody else on that table, like he was making the calls for someone else.

Sure. Sure, he nodded and approved.

With that, Karen and I were told to wait outside and they would bring Daddy out soon. He was free to return home.

I slipped into a bathroom while we waited for him. I was ready to burst. I had to get this out before I lost my cool in front of Karen. I didn't want to do that. This was her husband. I understood what that meant for her. I heaved out all the anguish and disappointment in that few minutes on my own in the bathroom, where I collided with the realization of what a sad life that poor Daddy of mine had lived.

I could see his life montage in my mind as I stood and wept at the small, metal sink, the water running so Karen wouldn't hear me. His sad beginning, losing his own father when he was just a little kid, a life of growing up in poverty, with a mom who saturated her despair in alcohol. Marrying my mom, the love of his life, and wasting it all, the two of them, the weight of alcoholism pulling them down most of their lives together.

The alcohol didn't simply quiet his pain, it *stole* every good and worthwhile thing from him. This marriage to Karen was a last-ditch attempt to get what everybody else had, but alcohol had taken over in this union as well, until cancer forced his sobriety.

Our stories had some common threads, but with a few big differences. Just like I had grown up without a mother, Daddy had grown up without a father. However, I had gotten to *be* a mother, while he had not gotten to *be* a father. Depression, anger, alcoholism, grief, bitterness had gathered up and run off with all the years of his life as our father. Wrecking relationships, neglecting to ever build them with his own family, Daddy lived his life as a victim of his circumstances. A life wasted by thinking that he was in this all alone and there was no way to peace or joy or goodness.

And that was the other big difference between us. I was getting to know God in a way my dad never did. I knew that there was a way out of tragedy, and that way was to look for God, listen for where He was speaking. I had gotten a new life since I had *heard* God speak. I felt His Presence in my life and I knew I wasn't alone. I wasn't a victim but a beloved child of Almighty God. With this knowledge came a new life for me.

Daddy had a chance to play a new role in his life. He had grandchildren and he wanted to *be* a grandfather. He had a daughter getting married soon. He was loved by three daughters who would accept what had happened in the past and leave it there, start fresh in the new beginning with him. If we could just have the time to walk out that new beginning together.

But now, cancer was the thief that loomed, intent on keeping us from crossing this new threshold. My hopes for us to be a "normal" family, a happy family, were pronounced dead on that procedure table.

On my white-knuckled flight back to Pennsylvania, to my own storybook family, I wrestled with God. Again, going back to the ultimate question of "Why God?"

"Why can't we just have this, Lord?" I thought.

"Why?" I demanded an answer, growing more and more angry at the silence of my Heavenly Father, who had lured me into thinking that He was "always there and always speaking."

"I am *trying* to remember that You are good. But this is not good. And it's not fair. And I haven't heard from you in a really long time," I protested silently.

It was a horrific flight. Not just because of my personal battles, but, literally, as well. The plane was packed full, with no empty seats and no space. Delayed several times, we sat eternally on the runway in our cramped little slots. When we did finally take off, it was late at night and a bad storm was raging. There was no "sit back, relax, and enjoy the flight" pleasantry from the captain.

"It's going to be a bumpy ride. We're going to ask that you remain seated and buckled in, for the duration of the flight."

There was so much turbulence, it felt like we were in a covered wagon hitting every lump and bump as we lumbered across the prairie. Except, we weren't in a wagon or on the ground. We were in a tiny, insignificant capsule suspended 30,000 feet in the air, being knocked around by the angry wind. The only sounds were the dirge of the engines as they labored to keep us out of reach of the violent air, the dinging of the seatbelt signs, and a few children, some crying, some screaming.

To be candid, I am a wimp when it comes to flying, and that night, I was petrified, considering how it would be just like God to take out two lives for the price of one. I could see the headlines, "Young mother dies in plane crash, leaving two young daughters behind."

I knew God all right. And He could be cruel. Casting off the peace He'd given me, I was holding Him accountable for this latest cruelty of terminal illness, along with the plane ride.

Had I lost all the hope I'd found in Him? It seems so. I mean, okay, *why* was God letting this happen to my dad? *Why* was God so silent as we begged and prayed for Him to give us a reprieve from this cruel end Daddy was facing? I was looking. I was listening. But I was not seeing or hearing anything from Him. It had been months since our last "conversation". Now, when I needed Him, He was nowhere to be found.

Didn't that fit perfectly with my initial impression of Him? Had I been fooled? I told you, trust was and still is, a journey I am on with Him. It's not as if I handed over the reins of my life and said, "Here. You take these. I'll just go along for the ride." I know there are people who do that, but I remain locked in a battle for control of those reins, temporarily handing them over on a case by case basis. I had tried handing them over for this latest need, but, He had neglected to show up.

Looking out the window, the opaque white fog swallowing all traces of sky, I heard Him.

He did one of those super-fast "downloads". In an instant, I heard from Him and in an instant, I had my answer.

"I don't want him (meaning my dad) to take comfort from anything in this world. I want him to look at Me for comfort."

And there it was. The "hearing" I had been waiting for. And in His God way, He had given me comfort even though this was certainly not what I wanted to hear from Him. In that moment, He confirmed for me that even in this seemingly out of control situation, He was present. He was sovereign. He was not surprised or trying to catch up to what was going on with us. He remained on the throne, and it was there that He directed us to come for comfort. Not in looking at drug companies and trials and doctors, although those things have their place, to be sure.

Jesus referred to the Holy Spirit as The Comforter. I get that now. The Comforter was saying to me, "I have this. I am here. And I am in control even though things seem out of control. I may not give you the answer you want, but I will answer you."

I felt soothed as I staggered off that plane and back home, to wait out another turbulent ride as we waited for the end. This was not the first time I waited for a parent to die. But, at least this time, I was fully aware of what was going on; I wouldn't be taken by surprise again. And this time, I knew my Savior. I was not alone.

My sister, Kellie, was married on a warm, brightly-colored October afternoon, just about a month after we got the diagnosis for Daddy. It was odd to be preparing for a wedding and, in the back of my mind, preparing for a funeral as well. But I was a realist and I knew it was coming. Shopping for a rehearsal dinner outfit on a tight budget, I wanted to find something that I could wear to Daddy's funeral, as well. It proved not to be an easy task!

Daddy rallied, sort of, for Kellie's wedding. There was no hope of him being able to walk her down the aisle, as he was now in a wheelchair. He was so weak, Karen sequestered him at the hotel until he absolutely had to be at the church. They had not been at any of the usual festivities surrounding a wedding like the rehearsal or the rehearsal dinner, or the pictures that morning before the ceremony.

It wasn't until I had marched down the aisle and turned to position myself to welcome my sister, the bride, as she walked bravely alone down the aisle, that I dared to look in Daddy's direction. I hadn't seen him since I left him a month ago.

He was right in the front, swimming in a tuxedo that swallowed up his body that was now enemy territory. His face so hollow and his mouth so protruded, he was unrecognizable. His eyes bulged out of his head giving him the appearance of being surprised, though he wasn't. Too weak to walk on his own, he was parked in a wheel chair at the edge of the altar.

There was no trace of the man that had been my father. He was already gone. What remained in the hollowed-out body was like a place holder for Daddy during this joyful event that was almost completely overshadowed, now, by the presence of Death that everyone could see in Daddy.

When we arrived at the reception hall, I was horrified to see Daddy with a beer in his hand, his prop for the afternoon. It was full and slopping over his bony hand as people inevitably bumped and flew by his wheelchair in the frenzy of activity that is normal at a wedding reception. It seems Daddy couldn't bear for his friends to see him looking so weak and unfamiliar, so his solution was to bring out the old Bart by holding a drink.

I think Daddy was truly panicked knowing he would be the center of attention at his daughter's wedding, instead of it being the beautiful bride pulling every eye to herself. Seated at a table and enduring the meal he could not eat, I am certain he made everyone sad and uncomfortable around him as they ate. Most people didn't have a status update on Daddy, but it didn't take any imagination to gather that there would be a funeral within days.

"They're taking me to the crematorium," Daddy said, as his buddies lifted him out of his chair and into the car for Karen to take him back to the hotel. It was his attempt at making humor where there was no humor - that old Irish trait.

Over the next few weeks, I called Karen every day, all day, starting at about 5:00 in the morning. I was getting "status checks" as often as I could without being annoying. I just didn't want this happening without me being close by!!

Daddy was admitted to the hospital about two weeks later, but Karen was downplaying it.

"He's fine. He just needs to get his feeding tube fixed. He's having trouble breathing, so they're going to give him some oxygen treatments."

"Do I need to come home?" I asked. I knew the time was coming but I couldn't jump the gun because I had two little children I would need to relocate somewhere, and a plane ticket to buy once the time really was dire. I wanted to be on time with this, but I couldn't afford to be too early. If this was going to be the last time I saw him alive, I needed to get there, pronto. But, if he maybe had a few more weeks, I needed to wait, so I didn't use up all my resources, of the babysitting and financial kind, too soon.

"No. He's fine Bridget. I'll tell you when I think it's bad," Karen reassured me.

A few hours ticked by and my phone rang.

"Yeah, you need to get on a plane and get here now," my sister, Marie, confirmed for me after visiting Daddy at the hospital.

And of course, with that input, it became urgent for

me to get home. I don't remember the logistics of how I got there or who was going to help watch the girls while Wayne was at work, I just know it all worked out.

Walking into the hospital, Daddy turned to look at me and his eyes were "disjointed". They were floating around in their sockets, one eye working harder than the other to be the anchor. He smiled and looked crazy with his eyes lolling around the way they were, and he immediately knew, upon seeing the "Out of Town Daughter", that things were bad.

"I must be dying," he threw out as a "joke".

"No, I just wanted to see you!" I said, which was true, but I hid the urgency of my trip.

I was so thankful that Marie had overridden Karen's assessment. I don't know if Karen believed the reports she routinely gave out regarding Daddy, or if she was just being protective. Protective of Daddy, of herself, of us. The motives were pure; I'm sure. But it's no easy thing to decipher from 600 miles away. Marie's alert had been accurate. Daddy was in the final stages of dying. All his organs were shutting down. It was a gruesome thing to watch.

Once, the nurses had requested that I stand behind the chair they were trying to put Daddy in, so they could lower him into it without worrying that the chair would move. So, I manned the back of the chair and as I did, Daddy's hospital gown came open in the back. I could see that there was fluid, and a lot of it, accumulating around his middle, sagging down over his emaciated frame, a result of his kidneys slowly shutting down. I felt sad that I had accidentally stolen a fraction of the small amount of dignity Daddy had left. I am sure he would have been so embarrassed if he realized I was seeing his bare backside. But, I don't think he knew. I think he was just that out of it, and maybe even beyond caring. I hope for his sake, that he was beyond caring.

That was the last time I saw Daddy. He died on November 21, 2000, a few days after I returned home.

On the pier at the lake house where they lived, Karen put a plaque that said, "The Leader of the Band played here until Nov 21, 2000."

It was a beautiful thing how Daddy had embraced that song. He saw it as a loving gift from us to him. What I had come up with while I was a young lost soul in high school - a way to stick it to him on my wedding day, became something we all cherished. Now, different words in that song stood out for me.

"And Poppa, I don't think I said, 'I love you' near enough."

Chapter 4
Orphan Spirit

Have you ever noticed that many of the Disney movies have the storyline of motherless children and orphans?

In many of these stories, it seems the greatest tragedy of all is the death of a mother. It must be an unfathomable scenario to any living creature because, per Mr. Disney, losing a mother is equally as tragic in the animal world as it is to humans. Think about all the main characters of Disney movies that experienced the death or absence of a mother. Belle, The Little Mermaid, Bambi, and Dumbo come quickly to mind and represent this theme. The orphan theme, those that had lost *both* parents, was prominent as well. Snow White and Cinderella fall into this category.

Yet in these tragically begun plotlines, life and brilliance are restored. True love is always the antidote for the loss these characters experienced, and happily ever after always comes. Mr. Disney shows us again and again his ability to make a beautiful ending from a painful beginning and we watch eagerly to see these stories unfold. But I lived this story. And, contrary to the animated version, it wasn't brilliant or beautiful. Birds didn't sing sweetly to awaken me. Mice didn't tailor my clothes for me, though I sure wish they had! No. Your broken, grieved grandmother wakes you up and your only clothes are your one pair of period jeans and a borrowed gray bra.

For me, after my mom died, this oft-portrayed storyline would have been represented more accurately by a smoking, devastated landscape. Annihilated by the removal of the mother, there is now only horrific brokenness in the dark, jagged remains. Smoke rising from the dust of the desecrated ground, rising around the shadows of what were once the foundations of homes, beauty, families and lives, now destroyed. The fog allowing nothing to be seen clearly. It is completely quiet now. No signs of life. As if a nuclear bomb just erupted and wiped out *everything*.

Looking at the sheer devastation, an onlooker would assume it was a scene where a war had been fought. They would never guess there was anything left but death here. No chance for anything to still be living. No chance for anything to crawl out from that scorched earth. Nothing could possibly be resurrected from the fallen ashes left behind here.

All those years after my mom's passing, I had felt like, and lived like, an orphan. It was about feeling abandoned, unimportant, unloved, belonging to no one. Now, with Daddy gone, I was shoved back into a battle with my orphan identity that I'd just begun to win. Daddy's death being so gruesome took my peace and called into question whether God's intentions and motives for my own life could be trusted. I took it personally - the way He had let my dad die. "*If* you are still good, why allow things to happen this way?"

My dear friend, Ruthie, was a lawyer who was often given the heavy task of removing children from abusive homes and placing them into a safe environment. Sometimes, this meant the children would be sent to live in a foster home.

Ruthie explained to me that there is a phenomenon with abused children, reported consistently by foster parents. In the night, under both the cover and the threat of darkness, these rescued children will frequently be caught eating out of the trash can. Though they are safe and cared for, they do not *trust* that safety. After all, they don't know the people they have been sent to live with. You can't trust someone you do not know. So, in the minds of these broken children, things could go downhill again at any moment. They needed to be sure they had plenty of sustenance when things did fall apart again.

Hoarding food, eating out of the trash, "toughening up", hurting the people around them before they can be hurt, these default behaviors are put into motion because the child still has the spirit of an abused child. Of an orphan who no longer "belongs" to or truly knows anyone around him. In his mind, he is on his own.

"You are alone. No one will save you," the Fear said to me.

Like the rescued child doesn't trust that they are safe, I readily picked that mindset back up, and the subsequent behaviors that came along with it. All those years I spent in childhood alone and vulnerable became my focus, because I felt alone and vulnerable again.

"Okay, God, *if* you are good and I can always trust You, then why didn't you make yourself known all those years ago? Why show up now?"

Doubt came in with one simple word - "if".

Yes, He could be good - *if* He decided to show up. He hadn't shown up all those years ago. Why? I allowed this tiny "if" to grow, untended, wild and big, and into destructive conclusions.

"You're on your own. You better do something because no one else will," was what I picked back up.

That one "if" caused me to shut Him off and allow Him in only on a "need to know" basis, unable to receive the goodness He wanted to give. Because, just like the foster kids, when you can't trust that goodness, you can't receive it.

As I unpack my journey of trusting God, you will surely recognize the tug of war game I'm in with God. "*If* you are good, then why __(fill in the blank)__?"

And really, that is the point. To show you that God was faithful to show up for me again and again, despite my continual backslide into doubt, distrust, and unbelief. He never withheld answers from me. He spoke to me at each turn, using my past experiences and the ordinary moments of my life to point out who He is.

My backsliding didn't surprise God.

Didn't the disciples of Jesus do the same thing? These followers of Christ prove trust is not an event; it's a journey. It takes a long time to get to know someone well enough to trust them implicitly. Trust is earned as you are shown over and over that it is safe to trust.

In both the gospels of Matthew and Mark, the same conversation is recorded between Jesus and the disciples. He had asked them who people thought he was.

"What about you?" he (Jesus) asked them. "Who do you say I am?"

Peter answered, "You are the Messiah, the Son of the living God."

"Good for you, Simon [Peter] son of John!" answered Jesus. "For this truth did not come to you from any human being, but it was given to you directly by my Father in heaven." (Matthew 16:15-17 GNB)

Yet, in just six verses, things change. Jesus has told his disciples that He will be put to death but will be raised to life in three days. Peter takes him aside and rebukes him. Peter *rebukes* Jesus!

"God forbid it, Lord!" he said. "That must never happen to you!" (Matthew 16:22 GNB)

Jesus understands that Satan has gotten hold of Peter's thoughts.

Jesus turned around and said to Peter, "Get away from me, Satan! You are an obstacle in my way, because these thoughts of yours don't come from God, but from human nature." (Matthew 16:23 GNB)

Even though Peter had, just six verses earlier, heard directly from the Father in heaven, he flopped right back to his old way of thinking, humanly and naturally, when he was confronted with something he couldn't understand and couldn't bear.

It wasn't just Peter. All the disciples had seen Jesus perform miracles first hand, but stumbled in their belief, their trust of who He was, again and again, causing Jesus to ask, "You of little faith, why are you so afraid?"

This could be translated, "You of little trust? Why do you doubt?"

What about the man in Mark 9:22 (NCV) whose son was possessed by an evil spirit?

"...But *if* (emphasis added) you can do anything, take pity on us and help us!"

And Jesus said to him, "You said, '*If* You can!' All things are possible to him who believes." (Mark 9:23 NCV)

Immediately, the boy's father cried out and said, "I do believe; help my unbelief." (Mark 9:24 NCV)

I don't know; I feel in good company with these eye witnesses of Jesus, who personally saw and spoke with Jesus, and could affirm His miracles. And yet, they, all of them, toggled between believing and doubting. Not that I want to be someone who goes back and forth between believing and not believing, but the point is that for all of us, solidly trusting Jesus, trusting God, is not a straight path, but a circuitous route, where we sometimes wander in distrust and sometimes walk with confidence.

We need not get stuck in that doubt or thrown off because we experience it. We need not be alarmed by our continuous journey in and out of the revolving door of trust.

God is not alarmed by it. It doesn't prevent Him from being good to us as we journey. He is happy that we wrestle, and don't give up, because wrestling is seeking.

Peter still became a pillar of the church. The believer/unbeliever's son was healed.

And I was given an answer to my renewed question of why did God take so long to show up?

When Lainey was a toddler, I received advice from some of the other young moms in my neighborhood. It was, according to them, time for Lainey Frances to give up the precious binkies that kept her calm through her days and nights.

Get rid of the binkies? Check! I can do that. Wayne and I agreed that was the Next Step in parenting Lainey.

I don't remember what story we cooked up about how this was all going to go down, but the Tooth Fairy was in there somewhere. We gave Lainey a few nights to get accustomed to the idea that the binkies' days were numbered. On that fateful night, we plucked the binkies from her mouth and her hand. You see, she had two binkies she employed - one to suck on and one to hold in her fat little hand and push on.

Everything seemed to be going well...for about 10 minutes...and then the wailing started. It was hard to listen to. She sounded wounded, like we had taken away her best friends. Because, well, we had. But, it was for her own good - right? It was time - my friends said so. And so it must be the right thing. It was Parenting 101 - "Binkies are bad."

Well, this wailing went on for over an hour, when *finally*, Lainey Frances got these words out, *"I'm not ready!"*

And that made something click for me.

It implied that, although she is not willing, not ready NOW, there will be a time when she IS willing and, thus, ready.

I looked at Wayne and said, "She said she isn't ready. Let's give them back to her for now." And so the rubber hostages were rescued from the secret place we had banished them and placed back in her hungry hand.

She did that sobbing, retching thing until she finally drifted off to sleep.

And I felt terrible that I had put her through all of this.

She wasn't ready. And I had caused immeasurable grief because I was operating on my timeline.

Please know that I am in no way doling out parenting advice here. But for me, for us, for this child, I feel that maybe if we hadn't given Lainey those precious binkies back, it would've left a different kind of scar on her than the crooked teeth we were trying to avoid. Ripping something Lainey deemed so valuable out of her hands could've paved the way for her to not trust us. It would've given her cause to feel that maybe she didn't know us as well as she thought she did.

"*If* Mommy and Daddy are good to me and love me, *why* would did they just steal my source of comfort?"

You can't give up those "self-help" behaviors when you only trust yourself.

Are you seeing this?

God will not do this to us. He knows the pain and pointlessness of trying to get involved before we are ready.

Nor will He *take* something from us that is ours to give up.

It's as we know Him that we learn, over time, to trust Him. Over time, we can surrender our self-soothing and receive His goodness. Now, we may not be able to articulate our readiness to Him as accurately as Lainey did that night for Wayne and me. But still, He waits patiently while He gives us room to figure this out.

And this is why I know God did not, could not, inject Himself into my life earlier on.

It's not that He wasn't present. He had been there. He just wouldn't force his timeline on me, because He knew I would reject it and a host of other damage would be done.

Two years later, after the attempted Binky Heist, my sweet Lainey Frances came to me to surrender them herself.

"I'm ready to give my binkies to the Tooth Fairy now," she announced confidently.

"Okay!! Let's do it."

She was on board with the plan, now. She was accepting that it was time to move forward. Lainey wrote a note to the Tooth Fairy, which I still have, explaining that she didn't need the binkies any longer. We put them in an envelope with the note which went under her pillow that night, and we waited expectantly for the Tooth Fairy to show up.

And boy, did she show up! The Tooth Fairy brought Lainey something even better than the tired, worn out little pieces of latex. The next morning, there was a lush stuffed animal in place of the envelope, a purple and pink soft cow, which Lainey named "Moo Cow Baby". The soft bovine was there to *replace* the thing Lainey thought was helping her but was really hurting her. The Tooth Fairy explained in a letter that Moo Cow Baby would help her sleep if she needed it.

When we are ready and when it is time, He will always give us something better to replace what we surrender to Him.

So, it all ended well. True, Lainey wore the "scar" of holding onto the binkies for too long. Her teeth were pretty twisted when they came in and, because she had incredibly slow baby teeth that were in no hurry to leave her mouth, she had to wait until she was 16 years old for the braces to bring her teeth into alignment.

Hmmmmm...She wore the "scar" of holding onto something too long. Don't I?

I wore the scar of bitterness and brokenness by hanging onto all the pain of growing up an "orphan", not ready to see that I was not alone.

Of course, Wayne and I knew that keeping the binkies would cause Lainey's teeth to be crooked.

But back in her room that night when she was only 2, we also knew there was a solution, albeit an expensive one. One we could not pursue until the right time. Braces would eventually fix the mark the binkies were sure to leave on her. We clearly knew it wasn't the best scenario, but it was what worked at the time. In the meantime, we wouldn't turn our backs on our precious child, even though we didn't "approve" of what she was doing. We simply waited for her to be ready.

God, not always approving of what I choose to hold

onto, and where I choose to get my comfort from, doesn't leave me either. Just as it would be silly to think that Wayne and I would abandon Lainey because this little child wanted to comfort herself with binkies, it is equally as silly to think that my Heavenly Father had abandoned me while He waited for me to see what I needed - Him!! God patiently waited for me, never leaving my side. While I wrestled with giving up the things that I thought soothed me, He was still present.

"I was there."

This answered my tired question of "what took you so long, God?" When I was ready, He gave me revelation through my own experience of being a parent.

He was there. I just hadn't seen Him. I was busy, distracted, doing things and holding onto things to make myself feel safe and comforted - eating out of the trashcan, so to speak. Quite simply, I hadn't been ready to see Him until I saw Him.

Just because I hadn't *felt* like He had been present for me, doesn't change that He was.

Not only does God remain with us while waiting for us, He doesn't withhold His goodness from us in the waiting.

For the foster children who take matters into their own hands, procuring sustenance from the trash, do foster parents stop providing for them? No, they continue to feed and provide for the scared child, waiting for them to learn to trust. Did Wayne and I keep goodness out of

Lainey's reach? No! Of course not! It would be silly to even think, as loving parents, we would keep any good thing from her while we waited for her to see things our way.

"I'm sorry, Lainey, but you can't have your birthday present until you stop sucking those binkies."

How ludicrous is that? I simply put the new stuffed animal away until she was ready for it, all the while loving her and providing for her in every way she needed.

Psalm 84:11 (GNB) says that God will not withhold any good thing from those who walk with Him. This is where getting to know the character of God is so valuable. The Bible takes away all that doubt and spells out clearly just who He is.

There had been goodness for me; I could look back and see it.

I had two sisters to ride the storm out with. There were some caring teachers who were especially kind to me. The long-sought friendships eventually came and are solid to this day. The right boyfriend came along and became the right man to marry. And of course, this family and this beautiful life we had were the most miraculous things that were eventually born from the mess of my tragedy. Even though I hadn't known or trusted Him, He still was good to me while I spent all those years, thrashing around, learning to trust, maturing to a point where I was ready to see. His goodness is constant, even when we aren't acknowledging of it. Some things He surely held back until I was ready, while His goodness continued to flow in areas where I could receive.

God creates beauty from ashes. It's what He does!! I

hadn't known this about Him. Isaiah 61:3 [8](AMP) speaks about God's desire to "grant (consolation and joy) to those who mourn in Zion - to give them an ornament (a diadem) of *beauty instead of ashes...*"

And that really is the point. God didn't leave me in my mess. He never does. Even before I knew Him or recognized Him, He was working on my behalf, busy with restoration and renovation. Just like the braces that straightened Lainey's teeth, God can always make beauty out of the things we have "messed up."

I can see that in my own life. Though I have made choices that have yielded some ugly consequences, my attentive Father has turned them all into beauty. The scars, because there are some, remind me of His goodness to bring beauty through a scar. They are now monuments to Him and His goodness.

Monuments? Sure! We look at Lainey's teeth now, which have been straightened and perfected, and we reminisce about the whole journey of the binkies and all the years of embarrassingly crooked teeth that she endured, and we always end the conversation the same way,

"But look at your teeth now!" And this is how we remember how the ashes have been made beautiful for Lainey Frances.

I look back and think of where I came from, and realize maybe Walt Disney was not wrong to show us beauty and brilliance emerging from those sad orphan stories.

"Look at my life now!" I marvel at the smoldering ashes God has made so beautiful.

There are physical scars and there are emotional scars and there is certainly pain in some memories, but even so, all of them can be regarded as monuments of His goodness - His ability and willingness to give us BEAUTY.

This very book is a monument to a once sad story made breathtakingly beautiful.

He *was* there! I am not an orphan. His goodness can be trusted.

Chapter 5
Change the Question

Lainey Frances was a very smart, inquisitive 2-year-old, and, like all 2-year-olds, her questions never started with anything other than "why?"

Driving down the road, I would hear this gurgley, funny little voice coming from the backseat, her mouth working the words around the binky that was permanently suctioned to her face:

"Why is that car blue?" she might ask.

"Because that man likes the color blue."

"Why?"

"Because it's his favorite color."

"Why?"

Ugh.

"Why did you sneeze?"

"Because my nose tickled."

"Why?"

"Because I have allergies and things make me sneeze."

"Why?"

Did she really expect an explanation of histamines and allergic reactions????

"Why is it raining?"

"Because there are clouds in the sky."

"Why?"

"Because God put them there," I tried to cut the conversation off by trumping it with the God explanation, not understanding meteorology myself.

"Why?"

Once, when Wayne and I were both in the car, she asked, "Why's the car moving?"

Wayne started in with a "dad" explanation, "Well, there are these little pistons that move up and down inside the engine. Oil and gas mix and blah blah blah blah blah...." he answered.

I looked back at her; her eyes were glazed over.

Okay, that wasn't what she actually wanted to know. She was not ready for a lesson on auto mechanics and the physics of why a car moves.

"The car moves because Daddy is pushing a pedal to make it go," I offered, giving her a more cognitively appropriate answer.

Silence. She was thinking this over.

"Why?" she fired again.

You get the idea. If you have children or are around children, you know they are relentless with the rapid fire "why".

From reading parenting books, I knew it was completely age appropriate for our 2-year-old to be asking "why" as her brain was forming new connections. I tried to be patient, but I confess I wasn't always. Often, I tried to head off the next "why" by anticipating what it might be and fitting it into my current answer, trying to barrage her with information and stun her into silence.

"Why did we turn around?" Lainey inquired.

"I made a U-turn because I can't go south on this road and still get into the parking lot where my doctor is. So, I had to turn around so I can go to the doctor that "lives" (trying to simplify and put it into terms she could understand) on this street so he can measure the baby in my tummy to make sure the baby is healthy so that when it's time for the baby to be born everything will be good because I want to have a healthy baby because I LOVE CHILDREN!"

Silence from the backseat.

"Why?"

"Lainey, it doesn't matter!" I yelled.

I'm not proud, but by the end of these relentless streams of "why" I was often frustrated and no longer entertaining her with the loving explanations that I started out with. The bottom line is - she was bugging me!

"She doesn't even understand what I'm saying," I would rationalize. "She doesn't really even *want* to know why! She's just asking 'Why?' 'Why?' 'Why?' like a parrot."

The point here is this: the child was a child. She had the brain capacity and the comprehension level of a 2-year-old. Limited in development, her brain was not yet capable of understanding most answers that were given to her, nor did she have the life experiences with which to interpret the matters at hand.

Our days moved along sweetly like this, answering Lainey's perpetual demand to know why, waiting for our new baby to be born. But without warning, things got scary, and our normal routine got turned upside down.

A few days before I was to deliver Emelia, I couldn't feel her moving anymore. I did all the things I knew to do. I ate something. I drank a cup of coffee. I laid on my side. And yet, I still felt nothing from this typically very active life inside. I called the doctor, the searing heat of fear rising through my body and the distinct taste of bile in my mouth as I got the urgent order from the nurse to get someone to bring me to the hospital right away.

"Mommy has to go to the doctor, Lainey. I'll be back soon. I love you!" I told her, kissing her and leaving her in the care of my sister.

"Why?" she, of course, responded, looking at me with her big sapphire eyes.

Was I really going to tell her why with her limited ability to understand the answer I would have given? Did she really *need* to know why I was going? Did she *want* to know why?

When I ponder these questions, in reflection of this potentially devastating scenario, my thoughts go back to the Tree of *Knowledge* of Good and Evil in the Garden of Eden.

Did Adam and Eve really *need* to eat from that tree? Did they really *want* to eat from that tree? No. They had only been lured into eating from it when the serpent, the enemy, convinced them that God was keeping something good from them. That was the turning point. They thought the fruit of all knowledge was something they were entitled to. They didn't understand that taking in this fruit would forever change everything.

By commanding that Adam and Eve not eat from that one tree, God wasn't withholding goodness from them. Rather, He was protecting them from the life-altering consequences that come with knowing too much.

"No, you don't need to know. You don't want to know. Trust me." This is what He could've been communicating through this one limitation He placed on them.

But they hadn't trusted. And instead of enjoying the bounty and beauty they had been given, they became focused on the one thing they didn't have. All too easily, they became convinced they were entitled to that knowledge. Look what became of that.

Just like Adam and Eve, we, like children, only *think* we want to know the answers, all the while, not grasping the consequences, the heaviness, that comes with the knowing.

And of course, Lainey didn't want to know the depth of what I could've told her. That I was afraid this precious baby, due to be born any day now, may not be alive anymore. That she may very well have breathed her last.

Telling her why I was going to the hospital would've stolen her innocence and trust of life, and would've forever changed her. It was my job to protect her, by not fully disclosing what I knew would harm her. I could, however, offer her a different answer.

What she really wanted to know was: Am I safe? Is everything going to be okay? Do you love me? Are you coming back? Will you read me a book and play "flower" with me when you get home?

To all those questions, I could reassure her emphatically, "Yes!"

"Yes, you are safe. Yes, I love you. Yes, I will spend time with you and do the things that I know you like, because I love you. And no matter what happens, that will never change."

Truthfully, I, too, was asking why that day.

"Why God? Why are you letting this happen? Why are you doing this?"

I see now that I was acting just like a 2-year-old to my Father, as I peppered Him with "why", not just that day, but for decades, refusing to move on until I got the answer I felt I was entitled to, the last nugget of knowledge I felt he was keeping from me.

"Why God?"

"Why did you let my mom die? Why did You let all of the goodness be taken from our family?"

Was God going to tell me why, with my limited ability to comprehend?

"No, my sweet child. You don't really want to know why. You won't understand what I tell you. The answer might scare you. But you can trust that I am good and will give you all of the things that I know make you happy because you are my child and I love you," He must have been saying to me that day of sickening fear about the sweet life I was carrying, and all those other days, as well.

Isaiah 55:8 (NLT) says, "'My thoughts are nothing like your thoughts,' says the Lord. 'And my ways are far beyond anything you could imagine.'"

To me, that verse had always reinforced the image I

had when I was young, of the elusive and distant God, harsh and unknowable.

"I know something you don't know and I don't have to tell you," was how I interpreted that verse. But He isn't like that at all. I had learned, now that I had heard Him, that He isn't dismissive or cruel.

I didn't say to Lainey, "I know something you don't know. Nah nah nah nah nah nah!" Right?

What God is really saying in that passage is just what I had said about Lainey.

"Am I really going to tell you why? With your limited ability to comprehend?"

He isn't withholding answers from us, because He doesn't withhold any good thing. Like children, we are not equipped to take in the depth of His ways.

Remember Wayne telling Lainey all the intricacies of why the car was able to move? That's us with the fullness of the truth that only God knows and understands. Therefore, He seeks to protect us from things we will not understand, things that have a weight to them that we are not equipped to carry.

Just as I protected my child from the permanence of knowledge she couldn't take in, He protects me. I may not get an answer to why. But do I really want it? Don't I really just want to know that I am safe? That everything is going to be okay? That He is good and I can trust Him to be good?

Decades of stubbornly holding to the question of "Why?" had thrown me off track. My unwillingness to give up this question kept me from moving forward, unable to consistently trust God's goodness.

And much like I offered Lainey a different answer, He offered me one as well, when I was ready.

I didn't know it at the time, but about three years from that day, the precious life that was lulled into a deep, deep sleep in my womb would love the book, *Tootle*[9]. That sweet baby, Emelia, would hand this "little bookie", as she called it, to my friends and crawl up in their laps to have it read to her. And reading Tootle was a commitment. It was one long Golden Book.

The corralled reader would be warned by me, "You don't have to read the whole thing to her. It's really long."

Now, the thing about Tootle the train is that he always wanted to leave the tracks and go exploring places that trains were not built to go. He wanted to go off into the meadow and look at flowers and frolic all day.

Tootle wanted what he wanted and took it upon himself to get it. Sounds just like Adam and Eve in the garden, right? How can a piece of fruit be bad?

"How could flowers and fields be bad for me? What could be wrong with getting a closer look?" Tootle might have rationalized.

But, trains aren't meant to go into the meadow. They can get mired down in the soft earth and become stuck, the sod mashing itself under their wheels, making them unable to move.

Of course, flowers and meadows are not bad in themselves. What makes them dangerous is that the little train was not built to handle those things.

The admonition of Tootle's engineer was always the same: "Stay on the tracks, no matter what."

I have learned that the question of "why" got me, and gets many of us, off the track and stuck, unable to move, unable to pull ourselves away.

Bringing Tootle to my mind, God was saying to me, "Sweet child, you really are looking at this all the wrong way. You are *limiting* what I can show you because you are stuck in the wrong place, mired down by the wrong question. My ways are above your ways. You won't understand the answer I give you. But change your question and I can answer you."

So, ironically, my new question became, "What should I change the question to, Lord?"

The bridge to this gap in my understanding came when a Sunday school teacher gave what I considered to be an impossible assignment.

"I want you to write down the pattern of God's faithfulness in your lives," he said.

Whaaaaat?

"Even David needed to remind himself of where God had been good to him," he prompted.

"Read Psalm 136 and use David's words to help you get started. Make a list and keep it. It will really bless you when you need some reassurance about God's goodness and faithfulness to be good."

"Well," I thought, "this is all great for all these other people in this class. They're lifelong Christians. How am I supposed to do this?"

This seemed like an undoable assignment to me.

But, in just the way God works, I was not able to put aside the feeling that I needed to do it.

"Okay," I thought. "But I have no idea what I'm going to write."

As I sat down to try and record tangible moments of God's goodness, His faithfulness to be good to me, I reluctantly invited the Holy Spirit to join me in this quest for sight to my blindness. Did He ever deliver!

I began to write. Stiffly and simply following the "formula" David provided, when steadily the Spirit began to give me revelation. What followed was pages of me writing nonstop.

The Pattern of GOD'S FAITHFULNESS in My Life

Give thanks to the Lord, for He is good,

Give thanks to the God of gods.

Give thanks to the Lord of Lords:

To Him alone who does great wonders,

Who through His compassion gave me hope each day I awoke as a motherless child.

Who dulled my pain until I was ready to take it on.

Who gave me two sisters who loved me all the way through.

Who kept me safe from a frightening, lost father.

Whose guidance was given to me as I chose a husband.

Whose hand protected me in my unthinking, dangerous youth.

Give thanks to the Lord, for He is good.

His love endures forever.

Who tucked Himself away inside my heart.

Who waited patiently for me, for many years, to come to Him.

Who never left me in any of the painful situations I encountered.

Who always gave me the strength I needed.

Who asked only to be discovered and loved in return.

Who gave me not one, but two beautiful daughters.

Who let me <u>be</u> a mother.

Who teaches me daily through the children He blessed me with.

Who gave me understanding that my journey is my journey, not covered up by anyone else's, only connected.

Who wants me to pray to Him.

Who wants me to learn about Him.

Who wants me to love Him as He loves me.

Who has known me forever.

Who has never given me anything I didn't come through.

Who looks at me as His child.

Who I scorn every day that I don't "get" how much He loves me.

Who never turns me away and gets "done" with me when I don't understand how much He loves me.

Who has shown His faithfulness to me through many bad places.

Who wants me to trust Him.

Who has pounced on my worst fear – breast cancer.

Who first prepared me to trust Him through and for the con-

frontation with my worst fear.

Who has opened my ears to hear Him more clearly.

Who put treasured friends along my path,

Who communicates with me more than I have ever realized.

Who has never left me.

Who wants me to know I am redeemed.

Who wants me to know He is good.

Who wants me to know His love endures forever.

Who wants me to know He is not mad at me.

Who talks to me and teaches me in ways I will understand (my kids).

Who knows my heart is bad but wants to be good but not totally (having trouble letting go of some things).

Who I am learning to accept and love and stop questioning: "Does He really love me?"

Who has shown His faithfulness to me: Job 42:12 (MSG)

"God blessed Job's later life even more than his earlier life....".

Who calls me by name.

Whose love I can never or will never be separated from.

Do you see? The issue had never been *why*!

The real question was *where*! I didn't know *where* God was all those years ago.

Where were you, God, when my mom was sick and my broken child heart was praying for her to be well? Where were you, God, as I was sent into a free fall after she died and through the next 18 years, like a pinball being shot through and around all the obstacles on a slanted, precarious playing field?

I finally saw what God had wanted to show me all along. God was *there* with me. I just hadn't seen Him because I was stuck, like Tootle the train got stuck, in the wrong place. Stuck by the wrong question, like a 2-year-old insisting on knowing why a car is blue. When you're stuck in a bad spot, but you don't know you're stuck, you won't allow anyone to rescue you.

I knew that stuck feeling. I'd been there long enough. I wanted to be rescued. I was ready to see what He wanted to show me, and stop trying to get what I wanted and thought I needed.

Then, like the engineer in the Golden Book did for Tootle, God cleared away all the muddy "whys?" that had been clogging my ability to move forward in my life, forward in my relationship with Him.

Rescued from the question of why, I was freed to ask, "Where?"

Staying on the track, seeing He had been *with* me faithfully, that was the answer I didn't know I needed.

"I was *there* then. I am *here* now."

In Exodus 33:14 (NLV), God told Moses, "I, Myself, will go with you. I will give you rest."

I got it. I could see that God, Himself, had gone with me. *Goes* with me. Knowing that gives me rest.

Life doesn't have to get derailed by the question of why.

"I don't need to know why," I find I must remind myself.

Can you imagine if the disciples had asked, "*Why* are you going, Jesus?"

What if they had dug their heels in until they got an answer to that "why"?

No.

"Where?" they had said. "*Where* are you going, Jesus?"

"I am going to prepare a place for you…."

Changing the question, changes the ability to receive the answer He aches to give.

"*Where* are you going, Mommy?"

"I'm going to the doctor and I will be back. And I love you."

"*Where* were you in this, God?"

That, He readily answered, as I wrote my list of His faithfulness.

Chapter 6
The Storm

When the girls were small, we were at the beach and I had just gotten them both to bed. I was in the kitchen, cleaning up from the day - putting things in order so that when I got up in the morning, the house would be clean and ready for the adventures of the new day.

It had been raining for a while, but nothing intense. I was enjoying the sound of the rain outside, not worrying.

Within minutes, the storm intensified and became fierce. The wind howled and furniture tumbled involuntarily across the porch. There was a phenomenal bolt of bright lightening, a tremendous crack of thunder and then, complete darkness. And I'm talking - black. If you've ever been near the ocean at night, when there are no lights, it's one of those deals where you think you'll be able to get a shard of light by opening your eyes really wide. It's kind of like trying to talk louder when you're attempting to communicate with someone who can't hear. Yes, exaggerating things always works.

Now, I am admittedly, ridiculously, afraid of thunder storms. I'm convinced they may, ultimately, be followed by a tornado. Even though I've never actually experienced this weather calamity, I have a solid understanding why I have remained, from childhood into adulthood, so petrified of the dreaded event. It has to do with growing up in the Midwest (a.k.a. Tornado Alley).

You see, in my cute little 1970s school, we had tornado drills like most kids had fire drills (we had those too). The deep bellowing alarm suddenly churned out its horrifying notification announcing a chilling menu of scenarios: there's a tornado coming, or there *might* be a tornado coming, or...we're just messing with you guys, but in any case, you'd better assume the position.

Like little ducklings, we dutifully followed the teacher down to the depths of the school basement where we were dropped off in the bathroom.

Now, get this, another one of those head-scratchers from my childhood. We little ducklings were instructed to squat under the line of sinks that were, for the moment, attached to the wall. Obediently, we crouched under our porcelain shields, our knees up around our ears, our hands clasping the backs of our heads. Just in case those sinks were torn loose from the wall, we would be protected by our little baby hands on our heads.

Oh my, so silly to think of this "plan" now. But you know, at least they tried. We never had a tornado, but we were prepared in successfully riding one out in the little girls' room!

Another success? The "Powers that Be" at school had bred in me an intense anxiety about tornados. As a child, whenever a springtime rain began, I was on active duty, listening to the radio in the kitchen, updating my family, who didn't seem phased by the rain. I knew, and still know, the difference between a tornado watch and a tornado warning. I was aware that just before a tornado whirls your house away, it will become eerily quiet and calm. Then, the funnel cloud will drop out of the sky, sounding like a freight train rolling through as it clears away your entire neighborhood, like a child clearing a game board of checker pieces, with one swipe.

I recall my mother was sitting on the Party Porch once with a girlfriend and, as they sat sipping their cocktails, I burst through the door to debrief them: it was raining, the temperature had dropped, and it was getting pretty quiet out there. All signs pointed to a tornado!

"There's no tornado, Bridgie. Go inside and play. You don't need to worry," she must've said to me.

Did I go inside and play? Nope! In what was strangely and disturbingly very much like a pagan sacrifice to the gods, I reported for storm duty in the alley alongside our house.

Now, don't get a picture of a dirty, scary alley where homeless people perch behind trash cans waiting to snatch little kids. Lots of houses in town were surrounded by networks of quaint, neat little alleys. The alleys alongside our house (there were two of them) were quite clean and, for us kids, they were really just an extension of our yard. Extra room to play in, you might say. At any rate, there was a storm drain smack in the middle of the T-intersection of where these two alleys met in front of our garage, and I quickly, inexplicably, made my way to it.

In an effort to appease the Tornado God, that I must have known lived in the drain, from what could only have been supernatural revelation, I began kicking stones and leaves and other alley debris into the drain. I thought if I could fill up the "mouth" of the tornado god, then this god would not reign down terror on us in the form of a funnel cloud.

Now, granted, I did outgrow the silliness of feeding the storm drain, but I still got an intense jolt of adrenaline whenever a particularly noisy storm grew up in my presence. (Hmm......sounds like some fisherman I've heard of!)

So, when this storm materialized that night at the beach, so loudly, so quickly, and with such ominous precision to take out the power in our neighborhood - the old, familiar fear fought to be acknowledged. But I was a grown woman now, with two precious babies to take care of. Straight away, I left the panic and got back into my Mommy-mindset, blindly feeling my way out of the kitchen.

"I'm right here," I said to the dark, and to the little girls who I knew had been jolted awake by the crack of thunder. I kept my voice calm, steady and constant. It would take me a moment to get to their room given the lack of light, but I knew hearing from me would comfort them while they waited.

"I'm coming," I said, in a silly voice, to lighten the mood.

"I'm right here. I'm right here," I continued saying, as I groped along the walls, eyes wide and crazily trying to catch a glimpse of light. Finally, I was in their room and on one of the twin beds where the three of us now huddled together.

"It's okay. Everything's fine," I assured them.

I gathered up these little babies and we carefully made our way into the master bedroom that held a king-sized bed where we could more comfortably ride out the storm together. We threw back the curtains and watched the supernatural light show, resting comfortably and safely, appropriately awed by the magnificence of the fury out over the ocean.

What could have been a really frightening night for all of us, instead, became one of our favorite memories from our summer beach nights. The girls still laugh about my methodical journey into the darkness of their room that night and my almost chanting reassurance. But they remember feeling cozy, not scared. And more than anything, they remember my words, "I'm right here. I'm right here."

In the fearsome glory of the storm that night, I understood something about God I never had before. Weren't my actions a picture of what my own Heavenly Father, the Perfect Parent, had surely done for me, all those years ago, when I was weathering the squall of my mother dying and, truly, in every moment since then? Hadn't He surely been saying, "I'm right here. I am right here."

He was there, just as I had been for my children. Surely, He had come straight to my side all those years ago.

How many times over the years had I thought, "It's awesome to know you now, Lord, but where were you then?"

"I *was* there," He was answering.

While this offers a picture of my children seamlessly relying on me, another storm, on another night, comes to my mind that told a much different story. On this particular night, Lainey was having a friend sleep over. We'd gone to the video store (this was pre-Netflix) and rented *The Borrowers*. With plenty of snacks, we headed down to our family room in the finished basement for a cozy night. As we watched John Goodman try to catch the pesky, wee little people, rain began to fall outside. It was dark now, which always makes a storm seem more foreboding.

Remember how I told you I knew the difference between a tornado watch and a tornado warning? Yes, this has served me well over the years. Our sleepover guests' parents, however, did not grow up in tornado alley and were not as comfortable with the terminology. It was for this reason that our phone rang.

"I'm coming over! There's a tornado coming!" the child's mom blurted out as soon as I picked up the phone.

"Really?" I asked, surprised. This was the first I was hearing about this.

"Yes! There's a tornado watch right now!"

Oh no, I thought. Silly, silly friend. "No, a tornado watch just means conditions are right for a tornado to occur. It doesn't mean there's an actual tornado," I said, calmly attempting to educate my inexperienced friend.

"No, a tornado's coming!" she was almost panicked.

"That would be a tornado WARNING," I assured her.

"I'm coming over!" Click. She was done with me, and I don't blame her. I picked the wrong time to go over tornado vocabulary.

Now, by this time, there were three little girls on the edge of their seats. They'd heard this tornado conversation and they were scared!

"It's okay, your mom's coming over to get you. Everything's fine. She just wants you home until the storm passes."

As I said this, there was a knock on the door and I handed the terror-stricken child over to her momma. Turning from the door, I saw my own two children were staring at me with their giant blue eyes round and wide with fear.

"Okay, let's go back downstairs," I said, knowing that if there were to be a tornado, the basement was the best place to be, contrary to my upbringing of crouching under a sink.

Now, we could've continued to watch the movie, because the power hadn't even gone out. But with every howl of the wind and scrape of the tree branches on the windows, the girls grew more and more agitated.

It was my youngest daughter, Emmy, who really got herself worked up into the lather that forced me to take action.

"Emmy, there's no tornado and even if there was, we're exactly where we should be. We'll be safe right where we are."

About this time, I fished a battery-operated radio out of the bare bones section of our basement that wasn't renovated. Once you opened the doorway to this area, you immediately left the comfort of the subterranean family room. A gray, cold cement room and lots of "stuff" was all that was on the other side of this door.

I turned on the radio, shocked that it actually worked, and was able to bring up a station that sounded clear enough that we would be able to get some sort of official word if anything was to change.

Still, Emmy sobbed and choked on her tears.

"Okay, Emmy, do you want to go in the back room?" I offered. "It's absolutely the safest place for us to be in the whole house because there are no windows back there. Nothing can happen to us back there because it's enclosed by cement," I explained, hoping she didn't take me up on it, because I really didn't want to go sit back in the cold cement "bunker".

But, that's exactly what the three of us did. The girls were convinced that, because our friends said there was a tornado, by golly, there was a tornado.

Back we marched to the bunker, the radio scratching out music, not a hint of the dreaded emergency signal that we would surely have heard if a tornado was approaching.

The concrete floor in our "safe house" was so cold, it made my pants feel like they were wet. Completely uncomfortable, and slightly annoyed, I continued trying to convince Emmy that we were safe; all was well, and there was no need to be waiting back here in the cold. I suppose sitting back there was Emmy's own version of feeding the tornado god; it made her feel like she was doing something productive to hold off the anticipated doom. The impending "What if?" But, I had my own comfort in mind, and I was growing weary of our hideout, so on and on I attempted to persuade her to believe what I was telling her, so we could emerge from this uncomfortable cell.

"Mommy, I love you. *But I don't trust you right now*," Emmy profoundly choked out between sobs.

Hiding in the stark, cold room, shutting ourselves off

from imagined trouble, Emmy believed what she saw and what she heard, not what I was promising her. She wasn't willing to trust me, the one who surely had earned that trust by now! Instead of this hiding offering her comfort, it was causing her more anguish. Truly, she was not hearing a word I said. And so, I simply sat with her in silence, aware of her fear but not able to do anything more for her than to be present with her and hold her tight.

In this silence, it occurred to me, didn't I say this to my sweet Father almost daily? "I love you, but I don't trust you right now."

I believe what I *see*, not what I know He has *promised* me. Instead of believing the One who has earned and deserves my trust, time and again, I put my trust in what I see or hear. Even with God consistently affirming His Presence for me, do I listen? No, I shut myself off from Him as I tuck myself away from imagined trouble. I may have seen I needed to stop looking back and asking "why" but I still had "what if" firmly in hand.

"I love you. But I don't trust you right now. *What if* something bad happens again?" I say.

"When this is over," I resolve, "I'll come out from this place and trust you again. For now, I feel safer in my confinement."

Hiding myself in the darkness of individual moments, even as years ticked by, I blamed His absence for the lack of light. But He hadn't been absent. Nor had He been hiding His goodness from me, as I had concluded was another possible reason for why things had gotten so bad for me way back then. No, to the contrary, *I had hidden from Him*. And like any loving parent would do, yes, even as I was doing with Emmy, He waited there with me.

Did I say, "Well, if you're not going to trust me, Emmy, then I'm leaving. I'll see you when you're ready to stop this nonsense!"

Of course not. He remained with me just as I sat with Emmy. Until she was ready, I knew my words were futile, but my presence was priceless. He had known that, too.

Emmy's attempt to save herself from the imagined trouble caused her so much grief that night. I could relate! I caused myself that same grief, trying to anticipate where trouble may come in. I saw it as my responsibility to prevent another huge hole from being ripped into my life from a random disaster.

What disaster??

Exactly. I didn't know. I had myself conditioned to be prepared for anything. Disaster preparedness was my habit. I regularly anticipated problems and sketched out ways to take cover from my presumed storms.

"If this happens, then I'll do this," I might devise.

Now, it wasn't like I consciously conducted these disaster drills throughout my days. But, many nights, once I laid my head on the pillow, my mind would go searching back through my day, to identify things I had done wrong or things that needed to be rehearsed. My adult version of "feeding the tornado god", I nurtured troubling scenarios, imagining the worst that could come from each one. Recall the time I tried to imagine life if my mom died. I couldn't imagine that scenario. Well, never again would I be caught off guard. If I could imagine it, I could prevent it. Or, at the least, I would be better prepared when trouble arrived.

To give you an idea of what this looked, I can tell you about one specific incident that wreaked havoc on my peace of mind for a few days.

Traveling with the girls one day, I pulled to the side of the narrow country road we were on because one of them was having a meltdown. I opened the large sliding door of my minivan so I could figure out what was going on. I made my way to the trunk to retrieve whatever it was I needed, leaving the side door wide open. As I came back around the van, a car came swiftly around the corner, very nearly hitting me. It would surely have killed me.

Instead of thanking God that, truly, His hand had held me back at that precise moment, I was tormented by the thought of my being run down by the rogue car, with the sliding door open to give the girls a full view of the tragedy. In my pre-sleep disaster preparedness drill that night, I was disgusted with myself.

"How could I have been so stupid to put us in that situation? I should've just waited until I was in a better place to pull over! Why didn't I just wait? And I left the door open! The girls would've seen everything! They would've been traumatized for the rest of their lives! What kind of a mother does that?"

I could imagine the gut-wrenching screams of my daughters as they saw their momma plowed down by the passing car. I could picture, perfectly, how they would look, strapped into the car, both with their little legs dangling over their booster seats, mouths open wide in screams of raw terror.

I actually went through this scenario over and over in my mind. Pictured it from start to finish. What would Wayne do? Who would take care of the girls? We had a life insurance policy on me, I rationally thought. Wayne could hire someone to help him. Would they move closer to family?

I finally slept that night, but I have long remembered the wrestling I did. To my mind, this near miss just reinforced for me that at any minute, life-altering tragedy can fall from the sky or careen around a corner.

The ultimate conclusion? Distrust of my Creator. He still couldn't be totally trusted. So, I had to pick and choose where I would trust God and where I would not. Deep down, I was always listening for the emergency signal. Being on high alert satisfied my need to be actively doing something to ward off calamity. But it never alleviated my fear or brought peace. It only gave birth to anxiety. For that is how anxiety is trained up, trying to anticipate and prepare for the unknown. It took a lot of moments from me. When I should've been trusting, I was afraid. When I should've been busy living, I was busy worrying. It's no way to live.

"I love you, but I don't trust you right now."

When fear and anxiety were my choice and my hiding place, He waited patiently.

"I am right here."

However, I choose to ride out the storm, He is there. Of course, it's His desire for me to come in close to Him, watch the trouble pass and come away with a treasured memory and firsthand experience of His nearness and protection. But even if I choose to hide or scheme, He remains with me, just as I had remained with my girls. He doesn't want me to wait fearfully, but He gives me the freedom to make that choice. He knows He cannot force us to accept the peace He holds out for us in His Presence. And just like I'd done with my daughters, He waits quietly alongside us. He may be silent, but He is never absent.

Chapter 7
Lola

I wish I was one of those crafty "Martha Stewart" kind of people. But, sadly, I never have been. My daughters paid the price for this in our early homeschooling years. There were no cotton ball lambs or egg carton flowers being made, no fun projects to speak of. In fact, the word "project" conjures up dread for me. We sprouted radish seeds in wet paper towels once, does that count?

When I heard about a chicken hatching project that the local homeschool group was offering, we decided to take the plunge. Compared to the radishes, this was going to be off the charts! We eagerly went to the meeting to pick up the eggs and the equipment. Farmer Jane gave us the basics on chick hatching. There were only a few things to be mindful of, and the rest seemed to take care of itself. Yes, this definitely seemed like my kind of project!

The first rule was: "Keep the eggs/chicks away from drafts." Easy. Common sense.

The second rule was: "Keep the eggs/chicks away from any family pets." Okay, another easy one. I can do this!

The third rule, and this was the one Farmer Jane got a little more emphatic about, was: "Do NOT help the chicks out of their eggs."

Apparently, the act of pecking out of the shell serves multiple purposes for the chicks. The shell sharpens their beaks and provides nourishment within its lining. Most importantly, the methodical pecking and working strengthens the lungs of the chicks. So, no matter how pathetic the chick may look, and no matter how long it took, we were not to assist the chick. In helping, we would actually be harming.

Finally, she cautioned us that if, by chance, any of the chicks hatched and were injured or less than perfect, we should put said chick into a baggie and gently place it in the freezer! Cover your ears, kids, this is heinous!

If, for some reason, we "chickened" out, and couldn't perform the mercy killing, we would be putting the injured chick at risk of being pecked to death by the other chicks. It seems the other chicks would have some supernatural radar for an imperfect addition and wouldn't be very welcoming.

I immediately knew I wasn't going to be euthanizing any chicks in my freezer. My chicks would all hatch just fine. There would be no pecking or gang fights in our incubator!

We returned home with all our equipment and our 20 eggs and set up the "incubation station" in the corner of our basement schoolroom. As was suggested, we numbered the eggs with a Sharpie and lovingly wrote a name on each one. It made the hatching so much more special! And then, we waited.

A few days passed when we got the first sign that the chickens were coming!! A pip and a crack in an egg. What an exciting way to spend a day! We were absolutely captivated by the chicks and their emerging presence. One egg hatched. A beautiful chick wobbled out after hours of chipping away at its embryonic home. Oooooh! Aaaahh! We diligently checked off the chart and logged which of the chicks had joined the party. And so went the day. And then - it happened.

Late in the afternoon, there was one chick that was taking an especially long time pecking away the shell. This chick was named Lola. We kept a close eye on Lola when finally, she broke through and stepped out. But in the fight to get free of the shell, she had a tiny little mishap. Still wet with the liquid from her shell, Lola was a little slippery as she got free. She stumbled and scraped her foot on a small, exposed piece of the wire grating. She was only slightly injured - no big deal, I thought. There was a little blood but certainly nothing freezer worthy!

However, because of her injury, Lola had a more difficult time getting dried off and acclimated. As she tried to join the group of fresh chicks under the heat lamp, they literally formed a wall with their soft downy selves, keeping her from the warmth she needed for drying her new body. They did the same as they gathered tightly around the food bowl, obstructing her from the dish whenever she attempted to work her way in. They'd all be huddled under the heat lamp sleeping, a quiet, feathery tapestry, moving steadily up and down with their breath, peaceful. Then Lola would approach and all of them would wake up and boisterously line up to keep her out. They screeched their objections and even pecked at her.

True, Farmer Jane had said the young fowl would reject a wounded chick, but *we* could barely see the small raw spot on her foot. So how did *they* know?

We took the matter, and Lola, into our own hands.

We'd beat them at their own cruel game. For three days, we kept Lola watch. We shooed away the other chicks so Lola could get to the food and water. Sometimes this worked but sometimes we couldn't keep the little flock away. When that happened, we picked her up and fed her by hand. If Lola couldn't get in front of the heat lamp to keep warm, we scooped her up and nestled her in our sweatshirts. We pulled her out of the group often to be sure she got whatever she needed.

With all the personal attention we gave Lola, she became special to all of us. We couldn't tell any of the other birds from one another, but we could always pick Lola out of the crowd. We weren't very good "farmers"; I'll give you that. We got a little too emotionally wrapped up in Lola's Plight.

When the chicks were three days old, we got to bring them back and it was none too early for me. What with the stress of the shunning and the unbelievable quantity of poop that was being produced, this little venture had lost its fairy tale quality. We brought the chicks back to Farmer Jane, explained that one of them was slightly injured, and prayed she wouldn't get the freezer treatment when they got back to the farm. And that was the end. This non-project mom could add a project to her resume.

I hadn't thought about those chicks in years. They came to my mind one day, when I was experiencing the dull, anxious sadness that liked to dance across my mind in the still moments. Melancholy seemed to be my default. It took vigilance and a lot of emotional energy to chase it away when it reared its head and I was exhausted from a lifetime of this cycle. Lyrics from the song playing on the car radio lit up for me. I was familiar with the "downward spiral of despair" the songwriter professed he, too, kept falling in. It seemed whenever I was left alone with my thoughts for too long, I easily fell into that downward spiral.

"When does it end, Lord? Am I ever going to get out of this pit and stay out of it?" I wondered quietly. "It feels like I climb out, only to fall back in."

"Remember Lola?" I heard, surprised to be getting a response.

"Yes," I thought cautiously. "I remember Lola."

"All right let me go back and see what I can pull from the Lola story," I thought.

Lola and I had both had troubles early on. Her physical wound forced her to be a loner. My emotional trauma was the doorway to my solitary state. In the years after my family struggled to kick aside the shell of death we all felt caught in, I thought of myself as damaged goods. Though most people couldn't see my injury, it was my identity. I hobbled into school with that identity.

"Hi. I'm Bridget. My mom died when I was 12," felt like a banner over my head. And like the chickens in the cage with Lola, the girls at school sensed my affliction. I felt the rejection. Being a chicken, Lola didn't care about the optics of being left out. She didn't care about looking like a loser in the chicken world. I, on the other hand, cared as much about being excluded as I cared about what my exclusion *looked* like to other people. My motive wasn't to be popular but simply to be accepted as part of a group.

To escape being publicly humiliated by the loner status. It's one thing to feel like a loser, and quite another to look like a loser.

I hung out at the end of lunch tables, grateful that I could at least perch there with other girls and not *look* like I was alone. I sidled up to them as they gathered in groups during gym class, hoping the rest of the class couldn't see that I was being cordoned off. I came alongside them as they gathered in groups in the hallway, at their lockers, and while they walked home. I focused, not just then, but for years after, on the fact that I was an outcast. I felt there was no place where I belonged. I felt unwelcome. Maybe I was or maybe I was only creating that perception because of how broken I felt. But the bottom line is, perception or fact, my life was steered by the identity I took on.

During the chick hatching, God allowed me to see what a helpless, battle-wounded creature struggling to get what it needed looked like. *It had been hard to watch.* If I was so disturbed by watching a chicken struggle, was God grieved by watching me struggle? Of course, He was. Stirring up this memory communicated to me that He had cared. He wasn't indifferent about my struggle. It must've been hard for Him to watch.

And all these years later, my sweet Father in heaven knew the root of this heaviness that routinely pushed me into that downward spiral of despair. Despair because I believed that the only one who claimed me had died. Despair because I'd been left behind, like an unclaimed bag, belonging to no one. Despair because it could happen again at any time.

Using Lola, God was assuring me, "I was there." I hadn't been alone.

But it wasn't Lola's struggle God wanted me to focus on. No. He was leading me to look at how I'd *responded* to her struggle. A profound understanding of the goodness of God came with this subtle shift of perspective: Yes, Lola was injured and excluded by the others, but this brokenness caused us to give her special attention and know her on a deeper level than we knew the other little birds. We spent a lot of time taking care of her. She may have been a reject in Chicken World, but in our world, she was the star! In the same way, my wounds weren't statements of disqualification, or stamps of rejection. Those wounds caused God to come in closer.

Focused on her hardship, I completely missed the *significance of the favor* Lola found with me. Likewise, I focused on my own struggle, not realizing it was because of the struggle that He knew me on a deeper level and gave me special care. I wasn't the Fat, Frizzy-haired Girl to God any more than Lola was the broken chick in my eyes! But wait a minute...

"Lord, as much as I love that You are explaining this to me, I have to say, I sure didn't feel special or favored in all of that mess!" So, that must be the end of this download. But you know, that Almighty and Gracious Daddy of mine continued to slowly feed me, offering me more insight. Yes, there were, indeed, similarities between my story and that of the fluffy fledgling, but I felt led to discover where our stories were different.

First, Lola had *allowed* herself to be scooped up and fed, where I had not. That frightened chick could've frantically continued to burrow under the squawking brood of chicks or pecked at my hand when I tried to extract her.

I thought of how my own daughters had allowed

themselves to be rescued by me during that thunderstorm at the beach. Instead of hiding under their covers, they heard me coming and *let* me take care of them. But me, all those years ago? I had burrowed myself into darkness, into the fear of being alone. I hadn't let myself be comforted. I hadn't listened for His voice, or even known to listen for it.

Another difference between Lola and myself was that Lola rather quickly learned to stop trying to join the group, and established her own little nook in the corner where she seemed quite content. But, for me, being alone and still was the enemy - a spotlight on the absolute hollowness I perceived within me and around me.

Not only didn't I want my loneliness to be seen, I didn't want to be left alone to ponder or experience the intensity of my depletion. Being alone had the power to suck me into a grief so profound I feared I would never be able to get out. The only way to avoid this black hole was to take up residence within the busyness of the world.

Preferring noise, I pushed into the broader world, mistaking the commotion and distraction it provided as comfort. I chose to fill up my life with what everyone else seemed to be filling up with. I embraced the role of being a party girl doing party kinds of things and accepted the consequences as part of a normal, full and fun life.

For example, in college, doesn't everyone get blackout drunk at parties, stagger aimlessly away from the safety of the group they're with, wander off campus into the country, wake up hours later on a golf course and not know how they got there or how to get home, just relieved there are no obvious signs of being raped or harmed? Sure, everyone does that.

No matter how many times scenarios like this, or worse, played out for me over the years, in my mind, it was better than the heinous quiet I would have to face without the risky behavior.

If I'd allowed myself to get still and quiet, even for a little while, maybe that's when God could've intervened. But I hadn't let Him. My destructive press for distraction was the equivalent of what would've happened if Lola had bitten the hand that tried to feed her. I wouldn't have been able to give her what she needed. Hadn't I kept God at bay in my life by desperately avoiding the stillness I needed to hear from Him? Preferring my own pursuits, hadn't I limited Him to shooing away some of the trouble, instead of being held in the comfort He wanted to give?

"I am not the author of pain," He whispered into this active contrast I was exploring.

"Yes! I see, Lord! I see it!" my heart replied.

God was not the author of my pain. Remember that temporary truce God and I had reached in my laundry room? When I'd come to understand my mother's journey and mine were separate? The permanence of that truce came when I realized that on my journey, so much of my pain had come to me through my own choices. And I can't have it both ways. I can't hide from God and be mad that I never saw Him. He'd been there. I can't create drama and trouble and hold God accountable for the consequences of my own bad decisions. He hadn't authored them.

I'm not celebrating the struggle or the pain, but I rejoice at seeing that the injury caused me to be closely held, and deeply loved, by the One who waited with me to be still and know Him.

Chapter 8
Object Permanence

There is a phenomenon among infants called object permanence. When an infant can see his mother, he is likely to feel happy and secure. But when the mother moves away from the baby, out of his sight line, most probably to do something *for* the baby, like prepare food or get a diaper, the baby gets panicked and thinks mom is gone forever...because he can no longer see her. Are you getting where I am going with this?

Just like an infant, we all get panicky when we can't see God working on our behalf. This is purely a developmental issue, a maturity issue. As the baby grows and new areas of his brain develop more fully, he understands that just because he can't see mom, it doesn't mean he is alone, abandoned.

In this journey of mine, I have often felt abandoned and forgotten when I couldn't clearly see God. Feeling panicked when I don't see God has proven to be a reflection of where I am in my spiritual maturity. I mentioned that I had some breast cancer scares in the past. Each time a mammogram came back bad, I descended into cold terror.

My last bad mammogram came shortly after I had the

blood test for the breast cancer (BRCA) gene. I wanted to take the test years earlier, but had been talked out of it because it could cause insurance issues. Once the insurance issue with this particular test was resolved, some doctors were encouraging their high-risk patients to get the bloodwork done. Certain it was going to come back negative, because I had that assurance, remember, I obediently laid out my arm and allowed the blood to be drawn.

I really thought nothing of it from that point on. I was confident that breast cancer had no place in my story. Peaceful in the sureness of God's words to me, "Her journey is not your journey."

So, it was like a punch in the stomach when I checked my voicemail one cold February afternoon and heard the message from my doctor. She wanted me to call her back and had left her cell phone number. I almost dropped the phone. I certainly dropped the peace I had. "Here we go, again, Lord. You said this wasn't going to happen."

With trembling hands, I dialed the number, not sure I would be able to speak. It was a snowy day and school had been cancelled. Apparently, my doctor's office had closed, as well, because she spoke to me from the top of a hill, where her own kids were sledding. I could hear their excited screaming in the background, which made this conversation feel surreal.

"Your test came back positive for the BRCA 2 gene," she carefully said, knowing what her words meant for me.

After that, I didn't hear anything but babbling.

When I was a kid, there was a Saturday morning show where a boy falls into a giant top hat backstage at a magic show. Once he topples into the hat, the camera angle changes, and the audience sees that he is falling into an abyss, with a red spinning circle in the distance, to emphasize the depth and chaos of his rapid descent. That's how I felt at that moment. Free falling into a swirling and inescapable abyss. Certain, again, the end that would eventually come for me would be tragic.

In my mind, the image of me with no hair, frail and sickly, immediately pasted itself to my brain. I could imagine myself in the cold exam room of whatever doctor was going to pronounce cancer over me. I could hear the words he would say, unemotionally and matter-of-factly, "It *is* cancer." I could feel my flesh being covered in goose bumps, both from my nakedness that would be covered with the stiff, disposable exam gown, and from the verdict he would've just given. I could hear the paper on the exam table rustling and ripping underneath me, as I twisted from the news, my legs heavy and dangling over the side. I could taste the tears I would be quietly manufacturing and see the images of my daughters and their tears.

"See, I told you!" Satan quickly sniped as I swallowed back the bile I could feel rising in my throat.

"You were right. I should never have trusted Him," we agreed.

The doctor prattled on about testing every 6 months, yada yada yada.

I was angry at myself for being lulled into a false sense of peace over this issue that had dominated my life. I had only, in the last few years, laid down this fear and handed it over to God to bury for good. Just like we'd waited for Lainey to be ready to give up her binkies, He had patiently waited for me to trust and turn this joy-stealing obsession over to Him. I had done that. Or, at least, I thought I had.

Now every "I KNEW IT!!!!" was coming back up with that bile. Like an infant who thinks mom has left for good because she can't be seen, I felt panic rising as I could not see God in this. I sat with my hand, literally, clamped over my mouth to hold back the sounds that were fighting to erupt from me. I had been fooled AGAIN!!

But like that momma who is still there, just out of sight for the moment, God was not gone from me. He wasn't angry at me for being afraid, but sympathetic and kind, knowing the road I had walked. Does a mom get angry with her infant, and say, "I was right over there, you ungrateful kid? I was making you some food, but forget it! If you don't trust me, I'm not giving you anything!"

No, a momma comes and calms her child. The first thing she does is pick him up and whisper, "It's okay. I'm right here. Look what I have for you," she might say, as she kisses and cherishes the frightened infant, knowing he is dependent on her for everything.

And that's precisely what God did for me in the coming days. After the panic and terror, after the crying out and the muffled wretches, so my girls wouldn't know my fear, when I got to a place where I was ready to hear, ready to be still, He was there to soothe.

There were no words that I heard from Him. Only a sense that He was still with me, still *for* me, everything was going to be okay. After all, everything had been okay for me, hadn't it? Hadn't He already shown me, through so many life experiences, that the key to finding Him when I couldn't see Him, when it looked like I was all alone, was to get still and remember His pattern of faithfulness in my life? It was my habit to pick up the old identity of the forgotten, abandoned child, but He wanted me to *remember* and *practice* my new identity, that of being His deeply loved, consistently fought for, and always recognized child.

Psalm 78 is all about *remembering* God's goodness. Over and over, Psalm 78 says about the Israelites:

"but they did not remember…", "they would not trust…", "they forgot what he had done and the miracles he had shown them…",

"they forgot the signs He did in Egypt…"

You see, when we are afraid, we forget to remember. The key to battling fear was to remember who God had been for me! I could do that! I *chose* to do that. When everything in me was screaming, *"RUN!"* I made the decision that I wasn't going to let my mind run wild this time. I was not going to forget all God had already seen me through.

The infant who cries in terror when mom's not visible eventually develops the ability to have an internal dialogue that could sound something like this:

"Oh, I remember this happening before. I can't see Mom, but she always comes back. She'll come back again."

And, as a child of the Most High God, I was developing this same ability. For me, it sounded like this: "I've been here before, Lord. You have always been there for me and you will be this time, too. *I will remember who You are.*"

In the book of Numbers, twelve spies had been sent by Moses to check out the land they were supposed to take over, the land God promised to give them. The twelve came back days later, and ten of them were freaked out by what they'd seen. They came back proclaiming how impossible it was going to be to take the land they'd been led to because the people there were giants.

However, two of the twelve, Joshua and Caleb, were faithful to God, *because He had been faithful to them and they remembered what He had already delivered them from.*

"It does look pretty scary. But God is with us, so we can do this!" they reported.

This felt exactly like where I was standing. Facing giants. THE giant of cancer. Here three parents, because my stepmother had wasted away from the dreadful disease as well, had been eaten up by the disease. And all three of us girls, Marie, Kellie and I, had been consumed by the worry and fear of it happening to us.

With this latest scare of mine, God brought it all into focus. It was as if he was saying, "My sweet child, learn to recognize the enemy and his predicable schemes in your life. He has consumed your thoughts and sometimes your very bodies. Don't you see how powerless he is in comparison to Me? You have got to trust me. Remember all I have done. Even in what seems bad, I am still good."

Romans 8:28 (MSG) says, "That's why we can be so sure that every detail in our lives of love for God is worked into something good." Even if the worst happened, I had to remember that God is faithful to work it into something good, as He had already shown me.

"I will remember who You are," I said aloud and continued saying. And God's peace flowed through my body. And, in the calmness that overcame me, some things became very clear.

The enemy had chased me my whole life with this same threat of cancer and I obliged by remembering the fear. I had not known the *power of remembering* all the good God brought to my life, the ways He had fought for me in my years up to this point. I was remembering the work of the enemy but not the work of my glorious and good Father in heaven.

I had to remember over and over to remember! "I will remember who You are, Lord. I will remember," I said aloud many times as I stood doing dishes, hands wet and sudsy, the terror causing me to go heart-pounding cold. It was a matter of transforming my life by retraining my mind that was so accustomed to seeing only the work and the patterns of the enemy. Remembering God and all He had done, like Joshua and Caleb did, reliably quieted my panic. Remembering calmed me and changed my focus, and I could logically lay out my choices about how to handle this new development of the genetic test results.

Was I going to get the preemptive surgery and have a double mastectomy? Opting to be a "pre-vivor" was considered extreme. No celebrity had publicly forged this path yet. I had a close friend, Mary, who had the surgery a year earlier, but still, it seemed radical.

Or was I going to wait things out, trusting God would not let The Bad Thing happen? Waiting it out, I would have to go for testing several times a year. I would have to live in that constant battle. I did trust Him and I felt that if I did have the surgery, it would be like me saying, "I am scared and I don't trust you, God. So I'm going to have my body cut up."

I wrestled with this decision for about a year. I went back and forth between having the surgery and letting things ride. I truly did feel peaceful about putting all of this in God's hands. I would know the answer when I knew the answer.

When it was time for the next mammogram, sure enough, I got the call that there were, again, abnormalities. I would need to come in right away for an ultrasound. As always, the ultrasound led to an MRI. The cycle of testing these lumps was familiar to me by now.

Face down in the MRI, the horrendous clanging of the magnets whirling around my body, the taste of metal in my mouth - a gift of the dye being delivered through the needle that pulled on my arm as the table moved in and out of the magnetic tunnel, I was repeating a line in my head from Psalm 91:1 (ICB): "Those who go to God Most High for safety will be protected by the Almighty."

The anxiety that was right there, right at the door of my mind, just waiting for me to open up and let it stampede in, was held at bay by me repeating this line over and over. I had more than one moment of thinking, "God, I can't keep doing this. It exhausts me. It's not that I don't trust you. But constantly doing these tests is distressing. It's hard to not get fainthearted."

Waiting for the results of the MRI was excruciating. I woke up in the middle of the night, exhausted from the waiting and the weighing of possibilities. I threw back the covers and stood up to shake off the "yuck" I was thrashing around under. That's when I heard an *audible* voice, next to me. It sliced the air at the foot of my bed.

"*You have cancer!*" it hissed. The word cancer had been hurled out with a very hard, over- pronounced 'k' sound. The second syllable of the word had been raspy and hung in the air with the ending 'r' sound trailing off into the air, never properly ending. The voice found me in the dark of my bedroom and I stood paralyzed and cold, covered in sensitive and tingling goosebumps. I felt the presence of the sinister voice as it hissed the death sentence over me.

"Jesus Christ," I quietly eeked out.

"I rebuke you in the name of Jesus Christ!" I said a little stronger this time. And it was gone. The feeling of that presence evaporated but I remained frozen in the same spot.

"Did that really just happen?" I thought. It seemed surreal now. Like maybe I had just imagined it. But, as I got some movement back in my body and groped for the dresser, groping not because it was too dark to see but because I was so shaken, I knew: that was real. That just happened.

Everything in the room was physically the same. Wayne was still sleeping and hadn't been disturbed at all by my momentary, intense spiritual battle. It happened and was over before I could comprehend it. But I remained chilled to the core and very aware that the enemy had just lashed out at me and had been chased off. I wondered, later, if that was the same voice we usually hear "in our head" and think it's just our own thoughts.

How had I encountered it so fully and physically?

I don't know if it was because I had been so entrenched in this battle about the MRI results and the surgery, or if my fear level was such that the enemy thought that coming at me "BIG" would be like the final and brutal punch that would knock me down for good, but I heard that voice in a way I had never heard before and I have never heard since.

I read a book called *This Present Darkness*[10] (Peretti, 2005) about a year before this pivotal night. The novel depicts a town locked in spiritual battle from the perspective of the *spiritual participants*, the angels and demons. When the main character in the book felt an undeniable evil presence in his home one night, he spoke the words, "I rebuke you in the name of Jesus Christ," cueing me to speak the same words. I felt I was standing at the edge of a spiritual showdown that must've been going on around me before I woke up. That would explain why I'd been so restless; I was responding to that energy around me. I believe there were angels surrounding me that night, holding off the demonic spirits that were trying to whisper to my soul. I had woken up in the midst of the battle and one of them hissed his poisonous message. The name of Jesus being spoken had ended the battle. The voice I heard is one I still remember and I know it was real. I was privy to the rawness of it that night for whatever reason. The impact the confrontation had on me cannot be overstated.

My answer came as a result of it. I felt, in that moment, my God was saying, "Have the surgery. It's a *gift* from me. Not fear from you. I don't want you to be in the crosshairs of the enemy with this ever again."

A gift? Having my breasts removed as a gift might sound odd to someone with a different history. But to me, I understood this gift as God was referring to it. The enemy would never be able to reach me in that old familiar place again.

True, it wasn't going to be an easy path. But living in fear those thirty-plus years was not living. He knew that.

Like any loving parent, He was working *within* the situation to give me comfort. Think of a parent who comforts their child after a nightmare and chases away the monsters under the bed. The child isn't scolded for being afraid or needing the reassurance that the monsters are harmless. This surgery was the equivalent of that. God was acknowledging my deep, deep fear of leaving my own children motherless, and He was graciously going along with what He knew, ultimately, was going to be the best way to disconnect that circuit of fear forever.

In the next few months, the preparation and research was done and I was prepared, even excited, to close out this chapter permanently. To live free of this fear forever, by the grace of God.

I sat on the edge of the cold vinyl chair, wearing the "Jiffy Pop" blue surgical bonnet, ensconced in the two enormous hospital gowns, the first open in the front and the second open in the back as I had been instructed. My freshly pedicured feet had been forcefully worked into the ugly compression socks with the grips on the bottom, and I was just waiting for someone to come and get me for the surgery. I was perfectly calm and ready, with no sense of being nervous or wondering if I was doing the right thing. I was so strangely calm, I whispered just under my breath to God, "Shouldn't I be a little nervous?"

Immediately, and I mean immediately, Psalm 23 (ESV) came to my mind. I knew the well-known first line: "The Lord is my Shepherd, I shall not want," which I was just going to repeat while I waited for my "ride". But, without thinking, I was reciting the whole thing. Nothing strange about that, right?

Except that I didn't know Psalm 23. I mean, I had read it, but I had never memorized it. And here it was just flowing from my mouth - the whole thing. John 14:26 (GNB) says, "The Helper, the Holy Spirit, whom the Father will send in my name, will teach you everything and make you remember all that I have told you."

Already chilly from wearing the hospital ensemble, I was covered with goose bumps and the absolute certainty that the Spirit was there with me, perhaps not visible, but certainly leading me through these verses, reassuring His child who knew that her Heavenly Daddy could fix anything.

Recuperating in the months to come, God remained with me. It was a long road, and though physically, there was pain, I look back on it with fondness and tenderness.

God and I grew very close in that time. One night, I remember beautifully, seeing the image of Jesus kneeling beside me, at the foot of my bed. I can't tell you if it was in a dream or if it was an image I saw during some of the hours of intense pain, but I know Jesus was in the room with me and I believe He gave me a glimpse of Himself, a little wink to me, a little pat on my head, letting me know so tenderly that He was in this with me. It was not lost on me that this very spot, where I saw Jesus, was the same place I stood cold and still about a year earlier as I heard the unmistakable voice of the enemy.

So, this battle with cancer, the fiercest one to date, the one I had dreaded and feared for more than 30 years, it blessed me. I had peace and victory where I'd been ambushed and trapped before.

Through it, God allowed me to *see* Him at work on my behalf, in an area I was certain He never was in. I heard from Him so clearly. In the constriction of the MRI, the night I truly believe I interrupted a battle, the day I supernaturally knew and recited Psalm 23, which by the way, I still recite regularly, and the night I saw Jesus at the foot of my bed.

I have been irreversibly changed from this whole experience. What the enemy intended to harm me with, God used for my good. He revealed himself to me over and over in it, and I was blessed in seeing Him, real and good to me, one of His only children.

And, true to Psalm 78, I continue to call on these memories and to remember who He is. I will give a good report. I will remember Your faithfulness to me, my sweet Abba Father, even when I don't see you. And I will do my best to tell the story You gave me, so that others can know your goodness.

Chapter 9
Food and Being Filled

We have a black Shih Tzu named Burford who loves peanut butter.

He will come running, from anywhere in the house, when he hears the unique sound of the lid from the peanut butter jar dropping onto the kitchen counter. He isn't fooled by any other sound; we've tried to trick him, for our own entertainment, to see if he truly can identify the Jiff lid versus other lids. He can.

He enthusiastically waits for the gooey delicacy every time! Staring at the purveyor of the peanut butter, his eyes take on a brightness that is completely irresistible. He prances in place, unable to sit still, his bushy tale wags and his whole fluffy body quakes in anticipation that any moment, the pasty treat will be held out for him.

Now don't be upset, but sometimes we just plain mess with him and put the jar away, close the cabinet and go about our business, trying to signal him that, "Sorry, there will be no peanut butter for you this time."

And yet, he remains. Excited, expectant, his gaze not diverted for a second.

If he could talk, he would probably be saying, "What? You're not going to treat me? You're not going to reward my dedication and belief in you?"

He doesn't give up. He knows it's a fake out. He always gets the peanut butter.

As I was being stared down and pranced around one day, watching him wait so expectantly for me to be good to him, it dawned on me, "This is how God wants me to wait on Him!"

He wants me to be undeterred by what I see happening around me, to not be put off by the blessing seemingly passing me by, but to stay focused until His goodness is, inevitably, delivered to me.

If the blessing doesn't come, I'm encouraged to ask, "What, Lord, You're not going to bless me?"

Like Jacob wrestled with the Angel of the Lord (Gen 32:22-32), earning himself the name Israel, saying, "I'm not letting you go until You bless me," He wants me to come to Him expectantly, unceasingly, waiting for His goodness, refusing to let go until I get it.

So, was I living that way? Was I sitting at His feet, like my little black dog sat at my feet, sure the blessing would come any moment?

Not so much.

You see, captivated as I was with Burford's peanut butter dance, I was a little distracted. I was presently being forced into a new season of my life, and I was not going entering in willingly. We were preparing for Lainey to go off to college. Emmy, too, was changing things up, and entering the public high school after having been homeschooled her entire life. Preparing to let go of both my girls at the same time, I knew big changes were coming for me.

Having put my professional career on an 18-year hiatus, I was going to be officially unemployed now that I was no longer the headmaster of the Anderson Academy. What I saw waiting for me were empty days without purpose.

Was I waiting expectantly for my Heavenly Daddy to bless me? No.

You can accept the transformative love He offers, as I had, and it will truly change how you live your life. But that doesn't free you from the temptation the enemy holds out for you to draw you back, into those old familiar places, where you used to meet him on a regular basis.

"What's going to happen to me?" I wondered aloud. I felt that familiar, nauseating feeling of being left behind, the 12-year-old on the stairs looking toward her dying momma's room, slammed by the reality that soon, I would be alone and aimless again. The thought of endless, lonely days, while everyone else was getting on with new lives, exhumed a fear in me that physically manifested itself in a pounding heart and an all-encompassing heat that kept me from thinking faith-filled thoughts. This scenario was just too reminiscent of "The Fullness That Had Once Been" before the beautiful, thriving tree had been ripped out, leaving me in the void that remained, looking at the evidence of roots left behind. Grieving what I felt I was losing and scared to go forward into the next season of my life, this threatened to be a sequel I didn't want to see. I wanted to keep believing for good things, but I was entering unchartered territory in my life. I couldn't see that there was purpose for me in this new season.

"I love you, Lord, but I don't trust you *right now*. What's going to happen to me? Is this as far as I get to go? Have I reached the end of my good days? I'm not so sure your goodness will hold much longer for me," the Fear spoke. And I listened.

"What makes you think you'll have anything different than he did?" bounced around in my head, in reference to my own father, whose body had been devoured in his empty nest days. Thoughts of Daddy's starved body always connected me to memories of food, and its role as a weapon of destruction upon all of us. It's here that I easily slipped under the surface of knowing where God had been holding me and I succumbed to the flood of memories fighting to take me down low.

The murky memory of myself, a child, walking home from school and crossing the threshold of the back porch into our kitchen. Always, there was a package of beef, wrapped in white butcher paper, defrosting on the counter, a talisman of the dinnertime ritual a few hours away. Sometimes my dad had to be gone overnight for work, in which case I could expect a light-hearted evening. But the thawing meat was confirmation that Daddy would be presiding over a family dinner tonight. Rather than being satiated, I knew I could expect the taste of bilious fear and dread during the meal that was threatening to come.

"Happy" hour was the precursor to the main course. When Daddy came home, he and my mom adjourned to the den, which was positioned at the front of the house, under a large tree that always kept the room cool and dim and dreamlike. They took their positions, my mom on the burnt orange, crushed velvet couch and my dad in his avocado green leather recliner. It was here that he would debrief my mom about his day over a martini...or two... or five.

By the time my mom was dismissed from the den, it was late - a "Murphy meal". Now keep in mind, neither of my parents ate anything during their "happy" hours. So, I can only imagine what an impact those martinis had on them. They took a toll on Daddy we could physically see. We girls swore eyes his changed colors after he'd been drinking, going from brown to hazel. He would carefully maneuver his way around the chairs, as any person who has had too much to drink concentrates very intently on moving without stumbling, while my mom brought the plates. An uncreative preparation of the tough meat was laid before us. Canned peas or corn was the closest we got to fresh produce, despite living in the heartland. The feast was, inevitably, rounded out with instant mashed potatoes and a small saucer piled high with Wonderbread, the piece de resistance of the meal.

And then, the fun began.

Who was going to be hunted tonight? Would it be my mom, one of my sisters, or would I be the lucky recipient of my father's attention? The hunter keenly honed in on the behavior of his prey and made his choice. For us, the chased, it seemed random. But Daddy was the expert. He knew how to choose. He thought Kellie and I were overweight, so I would frequently look up to see him staring at me, as I brought a fork full of food to my mouth. He didn't break eye contact, even if I did. The stare was laser-focused and came with a guffaw of some sort, a shaking of his head and a sneer. It was meant to draw the eye of his prey to him.

"Schooooooooooooo!" he would contemptuously, aggressively exhale, slowly shaking his head from side to side, never looking away. He wanted the target to look at him or cry or give some sign of noticing him as he continued his tyrannical stare. It was the first step of the dinnertime dance.

"You really think you need that? You think you should be eating that? You're already fat," he prodded the helpless victim.

"BART!" my mom would sometimes interject, but you couldn't count on her for this. Because we all knew the unwritten rules of the game here.

Rule #1 Never interrupt your father (husband) when he is doling out his disgust and disdain on someone else, lest it be redirected at you.

Rule #2 Always take the path of least resistance. Under no circumstances should you attempt to stick up for yourself.

If I sensed he was staring at me, I tried to keep my head down, and feign ignorance.

Therefore, the answer to his question would have been, "No sir," thereby agreeing that I should not, in fact, be eating, because I was too fat.

However, if you did decide to take such a stance, you were then expected to stop eating. And if you stopped eating, then you could be accused of being ungrateful and draw additional fire from him, which could take any number of twists and turns and lead to uncertain levels of aggression. There was no good answer or interplay in this game of Daddy's. So, you just hoped you weren't the "chosen one".

Far worse would be when he would get physical. That threat loomed there at all times, like a storm cloud just over the horizon. Would it make its way over the table?

More food memories piling on. My grandmother had been visiting once and just before she left, she made turkey fricassee. I hated turkey fricassee and could there be any reason why not to hate it?

It was a dish made of overly dry turkey and a gelatinous gravy poured over toast with some canned peas tossed in for good measure. It was hard to choke down the dehydrated turkey adrift in the slimy, thick sauce. You could chew and chew, and it seemed the masticated wad just got bigger as it swelled to a dry bolus in your mouth, refusing to go anywhere.

Marie was having a particularly difficult time with her portion, and since she was the one Daddy was staring at that night, he noticed immediately when she took a bite that he deemed too big to be polite.

WHAM!

He hit her across the face so hard she fell out of her chair.

"YOU PIG!" he bellowed.

Frozen in fear, with that turkey caught in my throat, I was bolted to my chair, unable to move.

"I've had it!" my mom screamed. With that, she disappeared into the infamous coat closet and re-emerged with her stylish mohair coat pulled tightly around her. We could see her in the kitchen, scooping up her purse and vanishing through the back door. She was gone.

And there we were, the privileged family in the beautiful home, our mother off driving while she was surely intoxicated, seething at how the man she married had not turned out to be who she must've thought he would be. *Left behind* to finish our meal in the "breakfast room", the groovy vinyl wallpaper with the colorful, psychedelic flowers indicating this was a friendly, cheerful place. But that was a lie.

Marie had dutifully gotten back into her chair and had begun properly eating the goopy meal, sure to cut petite bites, aware of how her bad manners had pulled Daddy's attention to her like a magnet. We forced the food into our mouths, silently, terrified there would be another round of the game. We listened for hints of escalation as Daddy defended his actions and consoled himself with hostile moans and groans, head shaking, "shoo-ing" and "sheesh-ing", the occasional profanity, and the ever clung to proclamation of "unbelievable" emanating from his small, curled up mouth.

Many times during a Murphy Meal, I'm ashamed to admit, I wished Daddy would choke on the giant piece of steak he was shoveling into his mouth. Then, we wouldn't have to live this way anymore. It was only a passing thought; it just passed frequently.

Wide awake in bed that night, I listened anxiously for my mom to come home. I was fixated on the terrifying thought, "What if she doesn't come back?" It's ironic the fear that kept me awake that night would come to pass in a way I did not imagine then.

These episodes didn't end when my mother passed away. They only grew scarier because now there was no one, absolutely no one, to possibly intervene for us. We were sitting ducks and we had to take whatever Daddy dished out, whatever he was feeling at the time, and be the objects upon which he displaced his rage and despair.

We discovered it wasn't just us kids who were at risk. No, Daddy never went after my grandmother, she seemed to have some invisible sign of "Off Limits" that even my mom hadn't had. But one night, he did go after her dog, Suzy, an energetic and, mostly annoying, Schnauzer.

Does being annoying mean the dog deserved the ferocious attack she endured that night? Certainly not, but she got it anyway. Daddy was particularly worked up this night and Suzy's waiting for food under the table was bothering him. In all fairness, I believe he fired out a few warning shots over the bow before he finally came unglued and lurched out of his seat, his chair thrust explosively behind him.

"COME HERE!" he commanded the dog.

He reached under the table, his meaty hand blindly groping for the slickly groomed animal. Suzy cowered at Mean Grandma Betty's feet, but even Grandma was smart enough to not get involved. She knew it would be dangerous to protect Suzy. Daddy got on his hands and knees and crawled under the table, recruiting us to help.

"Get her!" he bellowed, angry we hadn't offered our assistance voluntarily.

Shocked at this new low, and scared to disobey, we helped him trap her under the table, our legs blocking the way for her escape. Once he had her, he dragged her out where he could freely beat her without the encumbrance of the table. She tried to bite him, which only served to further enrage him, attracting more intense beating and swearing.

She finally broke free and ran off. As he was all set to go after her, my grandma finally intervened and spoke harshly to him, "Bart, no!"

He stared at her, repositioned the toppled chair, sat down, and began eating again. The sound effects, the head shaking, the muttering, it was all there, but the worst seemed to have passed.

Again I say, "...and everyone's okay with this?"

Okay, so we're all just supposed to go back to eating our dinner?

Yes. Pretend everything is normal. Nothing happened here. Foolishly, I thought, now that Daddy had beaten Grandma's dog, things would change. But nothing ever changed.

And this is where growing up with an alcoholic is really tormenting. Because, as onlookers and unwilling participants, we didn't forget what happened. I would always think, "Well, that has to be it. Something will change now. Someone will 'do something'. Someone will step in and rescue us."

But, the next morning, everyone pretended nothing happened, and Daddy didn't seem to remember, ever, the escapades of the previous night.

Since logic, accountability, and predictability were not found in our house, I never had any idea what to expect. Therefore, expecting the worst became my safest default. I learned not to trust what I saw. I learned other people would not protect me, so I had to rely on myself to get around unfortunate circumstances, which I did.

I learned to eat through the burning lump of fear and anxiety that, nightly, nestled itself in my throat as we took our places around the table. I learned to hold back, at all costs, the tears that were right there, ready to spill over and down my face, because if he saw me crying, that was a sure ticket to being the catch-all for his fury.

Eventually, I began my era of not eating, my way to get around my circumstances. It started out with just a cutting back. It gradually grew into barely allowing a morsel to cross my lips. In part, anorexia became a way to exert some degree of control over this scene, a way of saying back to my father, "I'm not going to sit at your table and eat what you're putting in front of me. You can control the purse strings and you can control the fear and anxiety that has become a perpetual companion for me, but you cannot control what I put into my mouth."

But for me, it was not just about control. Being thin enough was equal to being good enough. Being thin *qualified* me to be loved and to have the Good Life. Unfortunately, no matter how much weight I lost, it was still the Fat, Frizzy-haired girl who looked back at me from the mirror. This tunnel of control I built for myself as a way through grieving and sadness and ineligibility, a route to the Promised Land of acceptance and happiness, did not provide a passageway. It was empty filling up with empty. A taking hold of imaginary reins that offered no ability to steer or control, but I hadn't known that then.

Instead of delivering control, this obsession with food *took* control. It would be years of self-sought counseling, that I would start and stop and start again, before I could begin to eat and think of food in a healthy way. Before I would allow food to do what it was meant to do. Fill me up. Make me strong and nourish my deprived body that had become the unfortunate victim in my fight for control and eligibility, and ultimately, in my fight for an identity. It remained a struggle for me, to some degree, until I had my daughters. Having others to love and care for and think about does amazing things for the person who is inwardly focused, as I was, for so many years. One of the innumerable gifts my daughters brought with them is that they made life not about me anymore, and for that, I am so grateful.

When a baby isn't gaining weight, not being nourished by the food it's taking in, it's said to be experiencing a failure to thrive. Ironically, I sought starvation as a means to thrive. It is in thinking about these nightly episodes that I am caught by the irony of how food, which is given as a sustenance, a gift to nourish and satisfy, was the center of such twisted behavior for my family.

All three of us girls had been consumed by eating disorders. Tortured by either not eating at all, or, eating too much. *Consumed* in one way or another. Wasn't it ironic that my parents had died as skeletal remnants of what they had once been, their bodies starved? And their daughters, eaten away by worry and twisted relationships with food.

Food was the central theme of my failed attempt to steer around difficulty, as well as the vehicle that brought every member of my family down in some manner. It's funny, I thought in looking back, that it took me so long to let food in to do its job of nourishing and filling, just like it took me so long to allow my Abba Father in to do His job of nourishing and filling.

But wait a minute! That's the answer! There is a parallel between this battle with physical starvation and the starvation my spirit endured before I finally let His Love in to fill me up.

Remember how I looked for and wrote down patterns of His Faithfulness to me?

"If you look for Me, you will find Me."

Look for You where?

"Everywhere."

In the season of raising my daughters and getting to know my Abba Father, I'd been delighted to look at happy patterns, like my daughters and movies, as clues God was using to unveil Himself to me. Going down those "rabbit holes" had been fun, and exciting. But in following these upsetting childhood memories, it was like being limply dragged into the lair of the enemy, into a pit.

It hadn't dawned on me to look for my sweet Heavenly Father in these dark places. The epiphany came as I realized we have to look for Him in *all* areas of prominence, in the patterns and themes that repeat themselves throughout our lives, because He can speak to us in *whatever* holds our gaze.

Food was not randomly destructive for us. It was diabolical. Like he always does, the enemy perverted something good. For years, I'd listened to what he had to say about food. Here I was, listening again, as these memories urged me to disregard the goodness I already experienced and *expect* to be left behind, starving, and wasting in emptiness.

"Enough!" I thought. I had to bring God into these memories right now.

"So, what do I know about You and food, Lord? Do You speak through food, as well?"

I knew, throughout the Old Testament, the Israelites were fortified and replenished daily, with manna, while they were in the desert. They were commanded to have feasts, *celebrations of food*, as reminders of His goodness and faithfulness toward them.

I remembered God provided food for the prophet Elijah by commanding ravens to bring him bread and meat every morning and evening until the appointed time that Elijah was to move on. (1Kings 17)

"You went to great lengths to make sure your people were fed," I thought.

What about Jesus performing His first miracle at a wedding *feast*...a celebration with plentiful *food*? (John 2:1-11) There was another miracle of food when Jesus multiplied the loaves and fishes into 12 baskets overflowing to feed more than 5,000 people who had come to hear his teaching. (Matt 14:13-21) I mean, Jesus could've just stopped teaching and sent everyone away, leaving each one to find their own food. But He provided for them! And what about the little girl that Jesus raised from the dead? As soon as she arose, Jesus told those in the room with Him to get her something to eat. Surely that is evidence of His caring. His supply. His goodness.

"Your Father already knows what you need before you

ask Him," Jesus told the disciples. (Matt 6:8 GNT)

At the last supper, Jesus held up bread, broke it and gave it to them, saying, "Take this and eat it, for this is my body." (Matt 26: 26 NLT)

God said *He* is our daily bread and that he *causes* us to hunger, to teach us that we do not live on bread alone but on every word that comes from His mouth. (Deut 8:3)

It sure looks as though God uses food to speak - loudly. He is concerned with every aspect of our need to be filled. He knows what we need. He said he would use our hunger to *cause* us to seek after Him. He *feeds* and *fills abundantly*. There are no coincidences or insignificant details in the Bible. Food is important and given, literally and spiritually, in abundance, to those who seek Him. And at that moment, thinking about God and food together this way, it occurred to me that He had already caused me to look for Him, years ago, through food.

For example, does macaroni and cheese point to God? Well, yes, for me, it did, because of my dear friend Ruthie.

Wayne and I had traveled back to my hometown with our girls, who were both very young at the time, for a celebration of my friend, Crystal. The night of the big party, it looked like it was going to storm. As Ruthie stood at the stove, preparing the mac and cheese for the older kids, I stood right next to her - going on and on about my fear of my kids being afraid. Funny, right?

"What if the storm wakes the girls up and I'm not

here?" I didn't want them to wake up scared in an unfamiliar place, with an unfamiliar person babysitting them, and me nowhere to be found.

Ruthie said, "Let's pray."

"Okay," I thought, "I'll pray when I put the kids to bed." Because, that's when you pray.

But no. Ruthie banged the spoon she was using against the pan and set it down in the middle of the stove. She closed her eyes and began praying aloud.

"Oh. Okay. I guess we're praying right here at the stove," I thought. This spontaneous praying was weird to me at that point in my life, but if my friend wanted to pray right then and there, I was going to go along with it. I appreciated this lesson that you can pray anywhere, anytime.

I began calling these spontaneous prayers "Mac and Cheese" prayers in honor of the night Ruthie demonstrated this so powerfully to me.

Throughout the Old Testament, God instructed His people to set up monuments in order to remember miracles He performed for them. This "Mac and Cheese" title for spontaneous praying was just that for me, a monument reminding me that I can go to God wherever I am and no matter what I'm doing and I will find Him. The importance of praying was sealed for me then and there, but the clue about food I missed completely.

Another time God spoke the language of food was through my friend Kathy, whom I met when our daughters performed at a regional theater together. Kathy truly lived her life with Jesus all day long. She was so genuine in her love of Jesus. She saw the Father, Son and Holy Spirit in all things. Very naturally, she brought them into all our conversations. I had never experienced anyone living with Jesus this way, and I wanted what she had!

The childrens' cast were not set to begin for a few weeks but were asked to perform an unscheduled show for the local critics. I was worried the girls weren't ready. They hadn't rehearsed the whole show yet; this would be the first time performing all of it. Yikes!

"If the girls aren't ready, and they mess up, it could keep them from being able to perform in other shows," I said to Kathy.

"God doesn't set us up to fail, Bridge," Kathy assured me without missing a beat. "Even if the show doesn't go right, it won't be wasted. God will use it somehow."

"Hmm...'" I thought. At that point in my life, I still sort of thought He did set us up to fail, as a way to teach us a lesson. Keep us from getting too cocky.

The cast performed a flawless show and I was so moved by what Kathy had said and how she knew who God was and who He *was not*. It stuck with me. "God doesn't set us up for failure. What the enemy means for harm, He will use for good. He makes all things work for our good!" These are the conversations I was washed in, as we sat for weeks as chaperones at the theater.

Once, relating a tough decision I was making, I told Kathy I was confused about what to do.

"He doesn't give situations to confuse us, Bridge," she assured me sweetly as we talked things through. "He is the author and perfecter of our faith."

How powerful her summary of God's character and intent were for me.

As the show came to a close, Kathy wrote a note to Emmy, and encouraged her, "Keep God #1, Emmy!"

Reading that the next day, I thought, "Do people really do that?"

I didn't think they did. But wait! I had just witnessed Kathy doing that for weeks! It occurred to me that Kathy had God mixed into every moment of her day. Spending time with her made me see how I kept God a "side dish" in my own life. On the side, not mixed in with the "main dish". He was there for me on Sundays and in emergencies, but certainly not mixed throughout.

"Kathy has God mixed *in and throughout* her days," I surmised.

Given that she was from Louisiana, I thought it fitting to capture the lesson this way: "God wants to be a jambalaya!" I wanted to live with Him mixed all through my days.

There was that food connection again. But it hadn't come together for me until I was driving down the road that day - fearful God's blessings in my life would run out. In the precise moment I needed these ingredients to come together, the Holy Spirit stirred them up.

God had already been recapturing the enemy territory of food! Mac and cheese, jambalaya, a God that wanted *me* to be *filled* and my life to be *filled* ...with Him. There was God, circling and pointing in a heavenly, spiritual game of Pictionary. Food. Being filled. It was God that filled! And that fit. It fit the pattern God had already laid out in my life. It fit with all the ways He was already showing me He was there, mixed in.

Approaching an overpass on the highway, I saw that

I would be traveling straight underneath the bridge that rested above it, when I heard Him deep within.

"Why do you trust that this bridge will hold but you don't trust Me to hold?"

"True," I thought, humbled by the precise summary.

I go under and over these bridges daily, never worrying about them collapsing. Implicitly, I trust the man-made structures, subject to decay and mistakes, built decades ago by the Pennsylvania Department of Transportation.

But, I won't trust You to hold, God?

Fear takes. Faith gives.

Fear makes us blind. Faith helps us find.

Fear was taking my expectations for God's goodness to hold. Faith was giving me assurance that, unlike things of this world, He is not subject to mistakes or decay. Fear stole my vision for the future. Faith found the clues He was leaving.

There is absolutely no purpose in revisiting old, destructive memories and thought patterns, going down into those pits, if I don't mix my Savior and His Light into them. The Bible says the Holy Spirit will teach us all things and *cause* us to remember, in order to make everything Jesus has said understandable. (John 14:26) When my memory distresses me, I need to remember, too, that the Holy Spirit is there to help me remember who Jesus is, and make plain his goodness in my life, even the sorrowful times. Because now I *knew*, He could be found in those places too. He was there. He holds. He fills.

No, Daddy had not had a Good Life, a Happily Ever After.

"Why should I live this good life that I'm having revealed to me? Why should I believe it will hold, when I never saw it hold for anyone else? What about my parents?"

The answer is clear.

Because I know who is walking with me, *in the midst of*, the troubles that will, surely, come. And I know, He has deprived them of the power to harm me. (John 16:33)

Memories, passing shadows, of those meals where no one was filled. Memories of parents who died, their bodies and hearts weak and literally starved for filling.

But isn't that just it? They were starving for peace, for joy, for direction, for comfort. My parents walked blindly with no leading, no source of light or direction. Like I once had, they thought God was a detached, punitive god whom they could never please, and for whom their works would never be good enough. They knew the pain of their own individual journeys, struggles and mistakes.

They knew about Jesus but I don't know if they knew Him and accepted Him, along with the gift of salvation that comes with knowing Jesus Christ as their Savior. In Romans 10:10, the Bible says:

> *If you declare with your mouth, "Jesus is Lord," and believe in your heart that God raised him from the dead, you will be saved. (NIV)*

Had my parents believed and declared? I don't know. But I know it's never too late to be saved. Jesus is always waiting for us to turn to Him and gives us the freedom to take hold of the relationship with Him, up until our very last breath.

I think they didn't believe there could be more than a joyless life. They believed trouble was their lot in life. They didn't seem to *know* the Savior as the source of Light and Goodness with them in the trouble, and that, with Him, there is a way through the dark, to the other side.

King David captured this in my beloved Psalm 23 (ESV, emphasis added) when he said, "Though I walk *through* the valley of the shadow of death, I will fear no evil, for you are with me; your rod and your staff, they comfort me." But my parents seemed stuck in the dark valleys, not understanding Jesus had come to lead them through.

In Matthew 8, Jesus said to a man believing for healing, "Go; *it will be done for you just as you have believed*." (Matt 8:13 CEB, emphasis added). His Goodness hadn't been withheld. It was there for them. However, I think they believed for the dark valley and not the abundant life. Knocked about in life as they had been, it would've been logical for them to have been looking and believing for destruction. Why believe for something good and be disappointed, when they could infinitely expect bad things, and be "safe" with consistent sorrow? *They had what they believed.*

Is there a good life to be had? Speaking to his disciples, Jesus said, "The thief comes only in order to steal and kill and destroy. I came that they may have and enjoy life, and have it in abundance (to the full, till it overflows). (John 10:10, AMPC). What I think my parents didn't know, is that *life lived with Jesus is* The Good Life, the Happily Ever After.

"Why should I believe my life will be any different than theirs?"

Right now, going under this bridge, God was saying to me, "You can trust Me. I was there. I am here. I fill. I hold."

I believe for the abundant and overflowing life.

And I have what I believe.

In answer to my question, "What's going to happen to me?" was I waiting for God like my sweet pup waited for me? Excited and expecting to be fed with good things? Burford's expectant waiting, his wagging tail, revealed what he believed. He believed he was going to get something good. He sat happily and waited. And he consistently got his peanut butter blessing.

Or was I waiting as my parents waited? Wasted and wasting. They expected to live filled with troubles and heartache, consistently looking past their Father, preferring that which confirmed their expectations. They never had more than the physical and spiritual malnourishment they believed for.

Expectations *reveal* what we believe about God. We have what we believe.

The woman chronicled in 2 Kings 4 learned about setting expectations. A widow who could not pay her debts, with only a small bit of oil as collateral, her sons were going to be sold as slaves, as payment for her debt.

The prophet Elisha told the woman to borrow empty jars from her neighbors and pour the little oil she had remaining into them. As she poured, the oil did not stop flowing until the very last jar was filled to the top. After she sold the oil, she had enough to pay her debt and had plenty left to live on. The number of jars she gathered revealed her expectations. And she received what she believed.

And so it us with us. We either limit His Goodness to us or invite Him to bless us abundantly.

I choose to invite abundant, overflowing blessing by daring to put out plenty of empty jars of expectations and believe for His overflowing goodness to fill every one of them to the top and beyond.

The fear I spoke about, that was so present I could taste it? I could hold onto it, in lieu of believing for His continued goodness. Or I could do as Psalm 34:8 (NIV, emphasis added) suggests: "*Taste* and see that the Lord is good." (emphasis added)

Tasting reminds me that it is God, Himself, who wants to fill. The sad memories about food, the fear those memories triggered, were just passing shadows that scripture assures me I will pass *through*, not remain in.

I *expect* the Good Life, not because I am naïve to think there will be no storms, but because I know He remains with me and I expect His Goodness all the way to the other side. Circumstances in my life may change, but His grace is constant.

Reading *1000 Gifts* by Ann Voskamp[11], I was reassured when I read the similar experience she had driving over a bridge.

"I glance back in the mirror to the concrete bridge, the one I've boldly driven straight across without second thought, and I see truth reflecting back at me: Every time fear freezes and worry writhes, every time I surrender to stress, aren't I advertising the unreliability of God? That I don't really believe? But if I'm grateful to the Bridge Builder for the crossing of a million strong bridges, thankful for a million faithful moments, my life speaks my beliefs and I trust Him again." (151)

The Spirit speaks. His message doesn't change. He confirms His character and faithfulness so that all His children can know Him.

He can be trusted. He fills. He holds.

Have great expectations.

Chapter 10
I Open at The Close

I am drawn back to the present, leaving the memories that have come, in the midst of the awareness and appreciation I am feeling for church here in New York this morning. We are instructed by the priest to rise, as the communion offering is brought to the altar and I am back from my movie-style flashback, the breathtaking sanctuary now back in focus.

I am embracing the rituals I once rejected, along with the God I thought they pointed to. Understanding, today, the comfort embedded in those rituals, the comfort of His Spirit embedded within me. While I'm allowing God to fine tune all those old conclusions about sorrow and church, my daughter is downstairs dancing with a world-famous dance group, for crying out loud! It confirms for me the God I know now. The depth of His Goodness, and the way He spins beautiful pictures in direct opposition to the ugliness that tries to dominate but cannot. After years of wrestling, I see: *Fear takes beauty, but faith gives it.*

"Thank you," I say silently to my tender Father, whom I argued with this morning about attending. Still, despite my protest, He allows me to see that what I once avoided at all costs can be richly savored.

The mass ends predictably, with the priest's procession down the aisle, but I remain in my seat, taking in the last moments of the smells and hushed conversations. I meander by the baptismal font at the back of the sanctuary and imagine babies in long, white ceremonial gowns being held here, generations of families crowding around to witness the dedication. I am in the warmth and glow of an amber flame and I don't want to leave it. I'm putting off the stark reality of the June day outside. Like leaving a pool where you've been caressed by its warmth and gentleness, vulnerable and chilled once you step from the robe of water. This is what I felt sure would happen to me as soon as I stepped outside. But I was wrong.

Still wrapped in the power of the time spent within, proceeding slowly down the massive steps outside, I look up, as if from an ant's perspective, in awe of the vast size of the cathedral and the magnitude of what was imparted to me inside. Earlier this morning, I was sure the reason I hadn't met Him here was because He'd never been here. But that was not true.

"I was there."

The reason my family and I hadn't met Him is that we hadn't come here in order to *know* Him. We had shown up with our own agenda. We came to ward off trouble, presenting our attendance as an offering to hold off His wrath.

God is good *and* tragedy may, indeed, come. The two aren't mutually exclusive. But tragedy doesn't negate His Goodness, any more than a cloud or a storm negate the properties of the sun, still warm and bright on the other side of those clouds.

The radiant sun shines on me magnificently, kindling a different kind of warmth. I welcome it, as I step onto the sidewalk and propel myself through the strollers and tourists, through the folks who have somewhere they need to be and around the ones who don't.

Another movie is coming to my mind. Though surely not the intent of the author, the Harry Potter series has pointed me, in so many ways, to God. You see, Harry didn't understand his true identity, just like I hadn't. His parents laid down their lives for him, just as my Savior had done for me. He didn't realize what this sacrifice meant for him, unconditional love and devotion. He went through years of torment and self-doubt, along with tremendous fear and sadness. Sadness over what he had lost, his family, the grief of never knowing them, feeling cheated that he never got that chance. The intense fear of "He Who Must Not Be Named", the one who killed Harry's parents and left him an orphan with an orphan spirit. I knew that orphan spirit.

In this particular installment of the series[12], Harry's beloved teacher and mentor, Dumbledore, has recently died. When his will is read, Harry learns Dumbledore has entrusted him with the golden snitch that Harry caught in his first Quidditch match at the *beginning* of his time at Hogwarts. A line inscribed on the gift has Harry puzzled: "I open at the close."

What did this peculiar sentiment mean? Why had Dumbledore left Harry such an obscure, and seemingly pointless, gift?

After weeks of meditating on what the inscription meant, Harry finally understood: he had to go back to the beginning to understand how things fit together *in the present*. In going back to the beginning, he was able to understand the clues that had accumulated.

In the end, Harry encounters his worst fear. He is assaulted by the villain and left for dead in a sort of no man's land. But, he's not really dead. Quite the opposite. Instead, he arrives at an in between state, where he's finally free of the encumbrance of fear. He's ready to see, open to hear and receive the truth, because he has come to a place where he has nothing left to lose. He has, essentially, died to self, as the Bible would describe it.

He is met in this vast "in between", by Dumbledore. I truly relate when Harry asks, "Professor, is this real, or is it just happening in my head?"

"Of course, it's happening in your head, Harry. That doesn't mean it isn't real," Dumbledore replies, surprised that Harry would make such a distinction.

Our mind, the vast "in between", is territory we are so familiar with, we aren't likely to see it for what it truly is, the place where the battle is waged daily.

After this revelation, Harry goes through a sort of "rebirth". He is now ready to confront and unmask his enemy, to call him by his real name and disarm him. Naming things has a way of doing that.

We see Harry resurrected and eventually, taking hold of Voldemort's shoulders. The Boy Who Lived looks at Voldemort straight on, and says with his new-found wisdom: "Let's finish this the way we began, Tom—together." With that, Harry pulls Tom, who had only renamed himself Voldemort, into a full battle he, Harry, is no longer afraid of losing.

You see, it isn't until we go back, to the beginning, to look at the big picture, put all the stories and scenes together, knowing they have no power to harm us, that they make sense. Returning to the events from years earlier helped our hero, Harry Potter, know how to unlock clues that would help him defeat, once and for all, his enemy.

Despite the 90-degree day, I'm covered with chills as I understand. I had done just what Harry did. God had just taken me back to the beginning.

Like Harry ran from Voldemort, I spent years hiding from the looming presence of my enemy, the Fat, Frizzy-haired girl. I was desperate for distance from her. But the more I hid from the pain this unfortunate girl brought with her, the more power I gave that pain over my life. I allowed her to be renamed and avoided her at all costs because her presence kept me vigilant for the possibility of sudden and total destruction. She was a reminder to me that death and tragedy come unannounced. Her existence called up for me that heinous hole left in the wake of whatever catastrophe came or was to come.

"Even though you had trouble, it doesn't change that I was there. Look back at all of it, and see how it would have been different if I had not been there. When you look for me, you will find me," God was summarizing for me today.

The same is true for each of us. Everything points to God. Each frame of our story that we replay over and over is really a clue, a part of a bigger picture that leads us to something. The battle has not been random or just in our head. It has been real, and the stakes are high.

Psalm 34:4-6 (MSG) says, "God met me more than halfway. He freed me from my anxious fears. Look at Him...."

God *had* met me more than halfway all these years. He met me through supernatural events and through everyday things like movies and songs and thunderstorms, and in stories about chickens, to show me who He was. God made it clear to me that He had been there all along. And He met me here in New York, in the church where I was certain He he'd never been. He'd nestled into that creaky wooden bench right next to me.

"I am here now. I was there, too, my sweet child. I was there in the pain." The pain, I had avoided at all costs. "Look and you will see Me."

I see. I am seeing. The pictures are making sense.

In my search for relief and explanation of all the rippling trauma that came from that one event, I sought out counselor after counselor.

"I don't think you should hate her," one of the counselors said to me in response to my desperation to be untangled from the Fat, Frizzy-haired girl. "I think she should be celebrated. She got you up and out of bed and through each day."

It had been a turning point for me - looking at it from this angle. But it was only a partial truth, because, in fact, it was not that little girl who escorted me through each agonizing day after my mom died. She could do nothing of the sort; she was powerless. Here in the vast in-between, I see! It was my merciful God, my sweet Father, taking special care of me as I limped into school each day like Lola the chick. We went through it together. He was there.

It is God who gently took my chin in His tender, mighty hand and said to me years later, "That was me. I was there. Do you see me now?"

I used to have a sign in my kitchen that said, "It takes a long time to grow an old friend."

How true. Why are old friends so valuable, so cherished, and so hard to come by? Because they are the ones *you know you can trust*. Enduring hard times together *bonds* you in a way nothing else can.

"We've been through a lot together," these friends say to one another. They can rely on each other. Their relationship has been forged in the heat of intense trial. It has been sealed. It is solid.

In the same way, I am bonded and connected to my Father *in* the pain. *We* have been through so much together, my Abba Father and me. I can rely on Him.

In the book, *Into Abba's Arms* (Wilson)[13], the author relates how our pain is really like a wound. For the wound to heal, it has to be looked at – examined – so that it can carefully be cleaned out, for the balm to be applied and for the healing to begin.

We cannot ignore the past and its pain. Untended, it will be renamed and take on power it does not intrinsically possess. It will become an ever-growing, foul infection, something too ugly for us to look at, and will certainly overtake us.

Our Abba knows that when we are ready to look, we will see Him there. He waits patiently for us, knowing we'll have to clean the laceration together.

Do I have scars from my journey? Of course. But

scars don't hurt. Scars remain after pain is felt, right? The healing offered by God turns scars into monuments that *remind* me of His faithfulness to never leave me, to bring me through to the other side in victory. The victory of being a momma. The victory of having the family I always wanted to have. The victory of knowing I have not been left behind. The victory of knowing I am not alone; He is always with me. Has always been with me. He has always been with you.

Wrestling with my ghostly enemy in the genuine battlefield of my mind could be dismissed as unreal or nonexistent. The very presence of trouble could be a discouragement, an affirmation in my own mind, that God must not really care, otherwise there would be no trouble at all. However, the opposite is true. We have not been promised a trouble-free life. In John 16:33, just before he ascended to heaven, Jesus acknowledged to his disciples, that they would, indeed, have trouble in this world. But he also leaves further instruction to be of good cheer about the troubles they will face. "For I have overcome the world. (*I have deprived it of power to harm you* and have conquered it for you.) (John 16:33 Amp, emphasis added).

I had it all wrong. Walking through life trouble-free is not the blessing. Walking through trouble with the One who has deprived trouble any power over us is the blessing.

The battle has not been random or just in our heads. It has been real, and the stakes are high. It is a battle for our hearts and it will determine if we will actually know our Savior and the abundant life he died to give us. Or, if we will be consumed by despair, accepting the lies of the enemy, accepting the role and the identity our enemy has given us.

What I can tell you, reader, is what I have learned in my time spent sitting next to Jesus as He has written this book through me saying, "Let's make something pretty out of this..." is to not ignore the pain.

Look at it. Examine it. You are ready to see it now.

And you can count on Him to show up and speak to you. You might think you don't see Him or hear from Him. But you can, and you do. Whatever you have been walking through, He is there with you.

You see, He has *promised* that when we seek Him, we will find Him.

Through personal struggles and crossroads, I thought I had been walking through my life unescorted. But that was just another lie I believed. I was absolutely escorted. I was protected, and even, at times, carried.

And you are escorted as well. Even when you are not thinking about Him, He is thinking about you. Even when your thoughts are not focused on Jesus and His Redeeming power, His Presence is with you, nevertheless. He has promised to never leave us or forsake us - even when we don't call on Him. He is present. Even when we are not contemplating His goodness, He is still good. And He is good to us.

He is always speaking and giving clues, because He wants to be known. He isn't the author of your pain, but He allowed it to come to you. He did not stop it. Not because He is random and unpredictable, but because there is a purpose He will bring through it. He may allow you to be stripped of every earthly source of comfort *so that* you will see He is the only true source of comfort.

Tragedy is not there to rip an unfillable hole into your life. Nor is its purpose to bury you. Pain is allowed in order to point you right into the arms of your Daddy. He is talking to you. In everything, He is drawing, circling and pointing to Himself. Look in the everyday, seemingly ordinary for Him. How is he talking to you? Where is He talking to you? Is it through a movie? Is it through a song? Is it through the voice of a sweet child who says something profound like, "I love you, but I don't trust you right now."?

And when some time has passed and you are ready to see, you will be able to see Him with you. He was there then and He is here now.

Citations

1 Edelman, Hope. *Motherless Daughters: The Legacy of Loss*. Boston: Da Capo Lifelong, a Member of the Perseus Group, 2014. Print.

2 *It's a Wonderful Life*. Dir. Frank Capra. RKO, 1946. DVD.

3 *Medical Center*. Perf. James Daly and Chad Everett. 1971.

4 Brooks, James L. "Mary Tyler Moore Show - The Last Show." *The Last Show*. 19 Mar. 1977. Television.

5 *Three's Company*. ABC. 1977. Television.

6 Kidd, Sue Monk. "Chapter 1." *The Secret Life of Bees*. London: Tinder, 2015. Print.

7 Morpurgo, Michael. *War Horse*. London: Egmont, 2015. Print.

8 Isaiah 61:3: "To all who mourn in Israel, He will give a crown of beauty for ashes, a joyous blessing instead of mourning, festive praise instead of despair."

9 Crampton, Gertrude. *Tootle*. New York: Random House, 1972. Print.

10 Peretti, Frank E. *This Present Darkness*. Inspirational Press: New York, 1997. Print.

11 Voskamp, Ann. *One Thousand Gifts: A Dare to Live Fully Right Where You Are*. Grand Rapids, MI: Zondervan, 2010., pg. 151. Print.

12 *Harry Potter and the Deathly Hallows: Part 2*. Warner Bros., 2011. DVD.

13 Wilson, Sandra D. *Into Abba's Arms: Finding the Acceptance You've Always Wanted*. Wheaton, IL: Tyndale House, 1998. Print.

Made in the USA
Middletown, DE
17 May 2022